British Multipl

ANDY FLOWERS

Front cover image: 101689 leaves Cumbernauld on 4 April 2000 on a service for Motherwell.

Back cover image: Preserved HST prototype power car 43001 passes the 'Top Field' between Haworth and Oxenhope on the Keighley and Worth Valley on 4 May 2019. HSTs were originally designated as DMUs with power cars, though now they are widely regarded as locomotive-hauled stock. The HST set is hauled here by the brand new Class 88 88009 with 20031 and 47727. This location was made famous in the 1970 film *The Railway Children*.

Title page image: Class 108 M51935 awaits its next turn of duty (an evening 'Fish and Chip' special) at Bewdley, Severn Valley Railway, on 8 May 2007. Tragically, this car was severely damaged in a fire in May the following year and was later broken up for spares.

Contents page image: 156487 is at Newcastle on 15 November 2019 on a Northern service for Sunderland.

Key for tables

Unit Stock Carriage Codes			Examples	
B	Brake/Battery	DBSO	Driving Brake Standard Open	
C	Composite	DTBS	Driving Trailer Brake Standard	
D	Driving	DMBCL	Driving Motor Brake Composite (Open) Lavatory	
F	First	DMC	Driving Motor Composite (Open)	
K	Kitchen/Corridor	DMPMV	Driving Motor Parcels & Miscellaneous Van	
L	Lavatory/Luggage	DMS	Driving Motor Standard (Open)	
M	Motor	DPTFO	Driving Pantograph Trailer First Open	
O	Open	DTBSO	Driving Trailer Brake Standard Open	
P	Parcels/Pantograph	DTCL	Driving Trailer Composite (Open) Lavatory	
R	Restaurant	MBSK	Motor Brake Standard Corridor	
S	Standard	MLV	Motor Luggage Van	
T	Trailer	MSLRB	Motor Standard Lavatory Restaurant Buffet	
U	Unclassified/Utility	TBSL	Trailer Brake Standard (Open) Lavatory	
V	Van	TCK	Trailer Composite Corridor	
W	Wheelchair	TC	Trailer Composite Corridor	

Published by Key Books
An imprint of Key Publishing Ltd
PO Box 100
Stamford
Lincs PE19 1XQ

www.keypublishing.com

The right of Andy Flowers to be identified as the author of this book has been asserted in accordance with the Copyright, Designs and Patents Act 1988 Sections 77 and 78.

Copyright © Andy Flowers, 2021

ISBN 978 1 913870 59 1

Typeset by SJmagic DESIGN SERVICES, India.

Contents

Introduction

Multiple unit stock on the railways comprises self-powered carriages that are arranged in set formations. These do not require haulage by locomotives, but instead are powered by vehicles within the train formation itself, either in the form of undercarriage or within carriage power units or electrical transformers. In some cases, dedicated power cars can be utilised, usually at either end of the formation.

Multiple unit operations on British railways have a long and interesting history with an ever increasing range of types and methods of propulsion. The latter have ranged from steam, through electric, petrol and diesel and more recently battery and hydrogen power, together with varied methods of transmission of the power to the wheels, including mechanical, electric and hydraulic.

The many and varied companies providing passenger services have experimented with a wide variety of multiple unit types, generally as a more cost effective alternative to conventional locomotives and coaching stock. Over the following pages I hope to be able to give a flavour of the various types of multiple units that have operated in Britain, together with an insight into the future of multiple unit operation as the railways move forward through the 21st century.

Single self-propelled rail carriages known as railcars were the first alternative to traditional locomotive-hauled stock, appearing as early as 1847. These exotic new steam-powered vehicles were termed railmotors, without the space, by some operators, including the Great Western Railway.

The big impetus behind the expansion of multiple unit operations on Britain's railways came in the 1952 British Transport Commission report recommending, with a view to reducing costs and increasing efficiency, the replacement of push-pull steam operated branch line services with diesel railcars.

In the 21st century, even high-speed international services are formed of multiple units and, despite a recent slight resurgence in the use of conventional locomotive-hauled stock, the multiple unit is here to stay, at least for the foreseeable future, as the primary form of passenger train on the UK, European and indeed world railways.

Steam railcars

The first recorded steam railcar was a four-wheeled design named *Express*, which was produced by James Samuel and built by W Bridges Adams at Fairfield Works, Bow, in 1847. The vehicle was only 12ft 6in long but was put into service between Shoreditch and Cambridge for the Eastern Counties Committee. The railcar is recorded as running over 5,000 miles in its first six months so can be regarded as at least a limited success.

The following year saw Adams build another larger six-wheeled Samuel design named *Fairfield*, which was put into service on the Tiverton branch by the Bristol and Exeter Railway. In 1849, a third and even larger eight-wheeled design *Enfield* was built for use on the Eastern Counties Committee's Angel Road and Enfield line. This later railcar notably ran from London to Norwich in three hours and 35 minutes. Despite its clear operational capabilities, the vehicle was later converted into a 2-2-2 steam locomotive. Kitson's of Leeds designed its own railcar in 1851, which was imaginatively named *Ariel's Girdle*, although this does not appear to have operated successfully commercially.

With no further developments in railcars other than two examples built for the Great Southern and Western Railway of Ireland in 1873, the next major step in railcar development was an eight-wheeled bogie railcar designed by Dugald Drummond of the London and South Western Railway in 1902 for the Fratton to East Southsea branch. The design was a success and was followed by another example for use on the same branch, and two further cars for the line from Alton to Basingstoke. Nine more similar railcars were built between 1905 and 1906.

The use of railcars on a larger scale was introduced by the Great Western Railway, beginning in 1903. By 1908, 99 railcars had been built for the GWR and they went on to see use over a wide range of the company's branch lines. Of these, Kerr Stuart built 14 while the Gloucester Carriage and Wagon Company contributed eight examples. The remaining 77 were constructed by the GWR at Swindon Works.

A number of other railways also began to introduce steam railcars just after the turn of the century with 115 ordered between 1905 and 1906. The schemes were largely unsuccessful with their introduction gradually winding down, the final orders being three railcars for the Lancashire and Yorkshire Railway in 1911. The GWR's steam railcars had also fallen out of favour in 1917, and 78 of the fleet were converted to driving trailers for use in auto-trains (hauled by small tank engines) with the remainder scrapped.

Steam railcars began to become popular again in the 1920s with Clayton Wagon and Sentinel-Cammell supplying 74 railcars. These went mostly to the LNER but some were also used by the LMS along with the Southern Railway on the Devil's Dyke branch from Brighton. However, the introduction of diesel traction finally saw the end of the development of steam-powered railcars.

Hawthorn Leslie 1906-built steam railcar of the Isle of Wight Central Railway at Carisbrooke, this being numbered Railcar No.1. This was essentially an 0-4-0 steam locomotive with an attached passenger carriage, and it was reported as sold by the IWCR in 1918 before being retired and scrapped. Carisbrooke was the first stop on the line from Newport to Freshwater and the railcar is probably forming a service between the two. Carisbrooke was closed on 21 September 1953. (Andy Flowers Collection)

Ex-GWR steam railcar No.15 (Kerr Stuart No.0864) pictured in 1905. (Andy Flowers Collection)

Steam railcar No.93 is seen on the Great Western Society's 'Main Line' – the larger of their running lines, on 15 September 2020, hauling 1923-built Churchward non-corridor brake third 3755. The visibly narrower profile of the trailer coach enabled its use on the Metropolitan Line through to Moorgate from Paddington. The Great Western's steam railmotors operated between 1903 and 1935 and were the most successful of the type to operate in the UK. No.93, built in 1908 in Swindon, was one of the last batch introduced and, like many of the type, was converted into an auto-trailer on withdrawal in 1934.

Right: Railcar No.93 has been restored to a high standard internally as well as its exterior and mechanical parts. The hand straps for standing passengers are evidence that on occasions the units suffered levels of overcrowding. The seating shared some features of the trams of the time that the railcars were introduced to compete with on suburban services. The vehicle survived withdrawal from its auto-trailer role in 1956, seeing use as a study coach and then as a static office. After movement to the Great Western Society at Didcot in 1970, it was returned to service in 2012. The railmotor has even appeared on the main line in recent years on the Liskeard to Looe and Southall to Brentford branches.

Below: Sentinel-built Southern Railway steam railcar No.6 is pictured after withdrawal at Ashford Works. The vehicle was quite advanced for its time with an automatic boiler, enabling train operation solely with a driver and guard. The railcar was bought from Sentinel by the Southern Railway in 1933 for use on the Devil's Dyke branch near Hove, East Sussex, where it operated for two years. Passenger numbers proved too high for the small railcar and after a short spell at Westerham, where its reliability caused a number of operational issues, it was stored in 1936 and finally scrapped in 1940. (Throughtheireyes/Andy Flowers Collection)

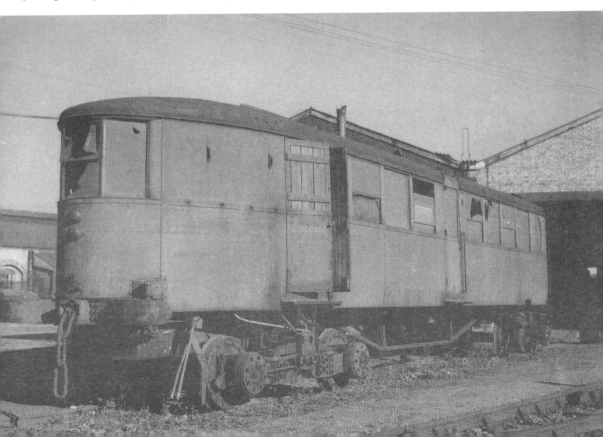

Chapter 1

The Introduction of EMUs

Electric Multiple Units (EMUs) are now the dominant type of passenger carrying rolling stock on the UK rail system, comprising over two-thirds of the passenger fleet in 2021 despite only around a quarter of available route miles currently being electrified. EMUs are typically formed of a combination of four carriage types:

Driving cars – with a driver's cab.
Motor cars – carrying traction motors connected to one or more axles.
Power cars – carry the equipment for collecting current from overhead lines or third rails.
Trailer cars – carriages with no driving cabs, power collection or distribution equipment.

Surprisingly, the electric multiple unit has a longer history of development than its diesel equivalent. The first EMUs introduced on the railway mirrored conventional hauled stock in design with wooden bodies and slam doors, though some early innovations were introduced. The initial sets in Britain ran on the Liverpool Overhead Railway from 1893 using 60hp Brown, Marshalls and Co cars that could be operated in multiple.

The invention of electrical control from a single cab by Frank J Sprague in 1897 had seen the EMU grow in importance and convenience, with London's Underground system replacing its smoky early steam traction; the Waterloo and City Railway leading the way in 1898. The London Underground system has a long history of operating electric multiple units but these are outside the scope of this book.

The Underground Mersey Railway began an electric service in 1903 with 24 powered cars and 33 trailers built by Westinghouse. The Lancashire and Yorkshire Railway later considered electrification of much of Liverpool's suburban network with a 625V four rail system, initially between Liverpool Exchange and Southport in 1904 using 600hp powered cars. Further developments included units supplied by Dick, Kerr and Co of Preston, powered from an overhead 3,500V DC supply.

In 1904, the North Eastern Railway introduced an EMU service between Benton and New Bridge Street with a 600V DC system, the network later being extended to form a circular route between Newcastle Central and Tynemouth. Meanwhile, the Midland Railway favoured overhead electrification, as used on the continent. It introduced EMUs on the Lancaster, Morecambe and Heysham Line in 1908, using two Siemens-powered carriages and a Westinghouse powered one, running on a 6.7kV 25 Hz system.

The Lancashire and Yorkshire Railway ran an experimental electric service between 1913 and 1916 from Bury to Holcombe Brook. The pair of two-car units employed were powered with Dick, Kerr and Co motor cars, again supplied by a 3500V DC overhead system. Following the trials, the Manchester to Bury route was electrified with a four rail 1200V DC system, opened in 1916, with the branch to Holcombe converted to the same supply in 1918.

The next year, the London Brighton and South Coast Railway used the same supply system for services from London Bridge to Victoria via Denmark Hill. The LB&SCR used three types of EMU, including South London Stock (SL), which were three-car sets until the removal of the first-class accommodation in 1910, after which they ran as two-, four- or six-coach sets. These were joined by Crystal Palace Stock (CP), which were three-car sets introduced in 1910, and the Coulsdon and Wallington Stock (CW), these being five-car sets built by Metropolitan Carriage, Wagon and Finance Limited, Lancing.

The LNWR built two extra lines between Euston and Watford Junction in 1907, with plans for through running on to the Bakerloo Line. The first electric trains began in 1914, running from Willesden Junction and utilising hired District Railway sets. Through electric services began from Watford Junction to Broad Street in 1917, followed by Euston in 1922. The 1914 units used were three-car sets powered with Siemens electrical equipment with carriage bodies from Metropolitan Cammell of Wednesbury. Following World War One, the electrical equipment supplier was changed to Oerlikon of Switzerland. South of the Thames, the London and South Western Railway introduced 660V DC third-rail services on some suburban lines from 1915 using 84 wooden-bodies sets built at Eastleigh between 1902 and 1912.

Following grouping in 1923, the new railway companies began to expand electric traction, particularly the Southern, with a third-rail system. Other operators favoured overhead 1500V DC electrification. For example, the Manchester, South Junction and Altrincham Railway, opened jointly in 1931 by the LMS and LNER, used the then-standard 1500V DC overhead supply, with 22 three-car compartment EMUs built by Metropolitan-Cammell to an LMS design.

The unique Glasgow underground system, a circular enclosed network, went over to third-rail electric operation at 600V in 1935, this using its existing stock converted from cable working. Soon afterwards, the Wirral Railway was electrified with a 650V DC third-rail system in 1938 using carriages from the Metropolitan Carriage and Wagon Company powered with British Thomson-Houston electrical equipment, giving access to the Mersey Railway.

After World War Two, other railways began to follow the Southern's lead with the LNER setting the pace with its 1500V DC Woodhead line and on the suburban lines out of Liverpool Street to Shenfield. The Tyneside Electrics 600V DC system was expanded in 1938 to South Shields with refurbished NER EMUs and new articulated units supplied by Metropolitan Cammell introduced on the North Tyneside Lines.

A 1948 British Transport Commission study into electrification recommended an expansion of the third-rail Southern network and 1500V DC on other regions. Notwithstanding this, the Lancaster–Heysham–Morecambe line was converted to a 6.6kV 50Hz system and the experiment was deemed a success.

Subsequently, it was determined that all future major new electrification schemes, other than the expansion of the Southern Region network, would be based on an overhead AC supply with the standard set-up being 25kV and 50Hz. The first line to be electrified with the new standard set-up was the Crewe to Manchester route via Styal, the success of which eventually expanded out to the whole West Coast Main Line and branches. This led to the electrified network we know today, including the East Coast, Great Eastern and Great Western main lines together with High Speed 1 (HS1) and soon to come HS2.

Future developments with EMUs are likely to include more hybrid types to enable operation over a wider range, including unelectrified lines. These are destined to include fuel cells, including possibly the option of hydrogen, with a number of hydrogen-powered vehicles currently in development. As technology advances and fossil fuels are gradually phased out, EMUs are likely to be the prime passenger rail vehicle for the foreseeable future.

The LNER electric units for the Tyneside Electric system were built by Metropolitan Cammell to replace the previous North Eastern Railway EMUs and they remained in service from 1937 to 1967 on the 600V DC third-rail network. A variety of vehicles were supplied including DMT, DTT, DMBT, DTC, TT and TC and sets were combined in a wide variety of formations. The units were replaced by DMUs when electrification was abandoned. One of the two-car sets passes Monkseaton during the last year of operation for the type. (Andy Flowers Collection)

Chapter 2

Diesel and Petrol Railcar Prototypes

The first viable non-steam railcar was built by the North Eastern Railway in 1903, this being a petrol electric autocar, with the Great Northern Railway following shortly afterwards with a Daimler-engined Kerr Stuart design. A number of different and often highly unusual types followed. For example, the LB&SCR also introduced petrol electric railcars in 1905, although these were not used for long and were transferred to departmental stock shortly afterwards. In 1914, the LNWR ordered a 90hp petrol electric railcar from Dick Kerr of Preston with an Aster of Wembley power unit and equipment supplied by the British Westinghouse Company. Like many steam railcars before it, the vehicle was eventually converted to an auto-trailer in 1924.

The development of more powerful diesel engines meant that railcars were able to haul trailers, adding further capacity and increasing efficiency. The introduction of electronic methods of control enabled railcars to be coupled together and worked by a single driver – the Diesel Multiple Unit (DMU) was born.

The Great Western used a petrol-electric railcar on the Windsor branch from 1911 to 1919, powered by a 40hp Maudslay engine with BTH electrical equipment. With a positive experience from this first tentative use of non-steam technology, the GWR trialled another AEC railcar, a standard Regal bus mounted on flanged rail wheels, on the line between Brentford and Southall. Experience with this vehicle, particularly the difficulties in turning it at the branch end, fed through to the development of a double-cabbed single railcar.

The GWR railcar production series prototype No.1 was delivered in 1933 with futuristic streamlined ends, no doubt influenced by the high profile streamlined express steam workings on the East and West Coast routes in the 1930s. After initial use in the Reading area in 1933 and withdrawal for some amendments, including braking equipment changes, the set re-entered service between Southall and Didcot and local branches in 1934. The success of this first unit saw the GWR order a follow-on series of higher-powered express units and the local and express types saw use with BR up until 1962.

Advances in diesel power and electric transmission in Germany and the USA saw increased railcar development through the 1930s before World War Two saw much of this use paused. Armstrong Whitworth supplied three Sulzer-engined 250hp diesel-electric railcars for the LMS, LNER and SR. The LNER unit worked between Scarborough and York with the LMS set used on specials between Euston and Castle Bromwich in February and March 1933. The Southern car saw limited employment and was sent to the LNER for services between Pontefract and Hull. The three railcars remained in service until 1939. Another approach was the rubber-tyred Michelin railcar, this being 10-wheeled and powered by a 27hp Panhard power unit. The set was successfully trialled by the LMS on the Coventry to Nuneaton line.

In England, the collapse of Beardmore saw much of its expertise pass over to English Electric, which went on to produce a highly successful range of 350hp shunters, some of which are still in use with their classic 6KT diesel power units. The Preston works, now taken over by EE, produced a trial railcar *Bluebird* using a 6HT 200hp power unit, which saw use by the LMS on its Market Harborough to Rugby line before transfer to the Bedford-Bletchley route.

The London Midland and Scottish Railway commissioned a 500hp four-car diesel electric multiple unit (the first in the world) from Dick Kerr in 1928, this utilising a Beardmore power unit of a similar design to that used on the ill-fated R100 airship. The unit saw use between Preston and Blackpool. The LMS also introduced a three-car unit in 1938 using two 125hp Leyland engines and a torque convertor for hydraulic transmission. The unit was based at Bedford and the first line to see regular use by the railcar was that between Oxford and Cambridge. With generated revenue being disappointing, the set was transferred to the St Pancras-Bedford stoppers, occasionally running through to Nottingham.

Internal combustion technology advanced following World War Two with more powerful diesel engines becoming available for rail use, though it was the success of the Great Western Railway railcars, particularly their use in paired sets, that eventually laid the groundwork for the mass introduction of the First Generation DMUs by BR in the 1950s.

The North Eastern Railway experimented with electric transmission with two petrol-powered railcars (termed autocars) built at its carriage works in York in 1903. The technology would go on to become very successful and in many ways was the forerunner of the diesel electric transmission system now in use worldwide. The two railcars, numbered 3170 and 3171, were powered by successively more powerful engines, initially an 85hp Napier, which were replaced in 1904 by 92hp Wolseley engines. Then in 1923, No. 3170 was fitted with a 225hp engine, which enabled it to haul unpowered coaches, heralding a new style of railway operation – the multiple unit. Their maximum speed was 36 mph and the units saw use mostly around Scarborough, Selby and Harrogate. 3170 was rescued from being used as a holiday home and after award-winning restoration work between 2011 and 2018 (which included a conversion to diesel power), the railcar re-entered service at the Bolton and Embsay Railway. The unit is seen at Loughborough on the Great Central Railway in 2019.

The London Brighton and South Coast Railway introduced petrol electric railcars for branch line services, including Kemp Town and Pevensey, between 1905 and 1911. Following their withdrawal from passenger service, they were transferred to Peckham Rye depot to be used as maintenance vehicles for the overhead wiring; the LB&SCR taking a different approach to electrification from its pre-grouping neighbours, which favoured third-rail supply. Two of the cars are seen on the depot in 1927. (Andy Flowers Collection)

On 22 April 2011, GWR diesel railcar No.22 is working the short demonstration line at the Great Western Society's Didcot base. The adjoining line is dual gauge (standard and broad gauge) to enable use of the 2005-built broad gauge GWR steam replica *Fire Fly*. The single-car diesel railcar was built in 1940 and is powered by two AEC power units of 105hp each, this being of a similar type to those used in London Transport's Routemaster buses. After withdrawal from service in 1962, and storage at Swindon Works, the railcar was preserved for use on the Severn Valley Railway, transferring to Didcot in 1978.

On 11 September 2020, GWR diesel railcar No.4 takes pride of place in the Great Hall at the National Railway Museum. Built by Park Royal in 1934, this unit belongs to one of the earlier, more-powerful streamlined batches of GWR railcars, nicknamed 'flying bananas'. Powered by two AEC 130hp power units, this gave a top speed of 75mph and enabled use on a high-speed service between Birmingham and Cardiff. The unit was transferred into preservation at Swindon in 1963 and after a spell at Didcot was transferred into the National Collection at York in 1979.

Waggon und Maschinenbau railbus E79960 is seen at Preston (on the Ribble Railway) on 30 September 2017 awaiting its next turn of duty. The 55mph-limited unit is painted in the popular BR green livery with the, optimistically termed, 'speed whiskers'. The unit was preserved as long ago as 1967 after many of the branch lines that the fleet was used on were closed after the Beeching Report and became one of the early acquisitions of the North Norfolk Railway. The unit, one of five built in Germany in 1958, is currently on a long-term loan from the NNR to the Ribble Steam Railway.

Chapter 3

First Generation Overhead EMUs

O n its formation in 1948, British Railways inherited a wide range of electrified stock with no general standardisation, even for supply type and voltages. A 1951 report recommended further electrification based on the LNER's 1500V DC system, pioneered by the MSJA in 1931. British Railways' first electrification schemes carried on from those initially planned by the LNER using the agreed 1500V DC system (the Woodhead route and suburban lines out of Liverpool Street) with its first EMUs to be introduced under nationalisation being the Class 306 Shenfield units and the Class 506 Hadfield units.

Following the results of the BTC's Modernisation Plan and the decision to replace the steam fleet with a mixture of diesel and electric locomotives and multiple unit stock, for its new fleet of EMUs, British Railways decided on three main designs. These included high-density suburban EMUs with no toilets or through access between vehicles, and outer suburban EMUs with some first-class accommodation and toilet facilities but still non-gangwayed. Lastly, there were to be express passenger EMUs that would be similar to convention locomotive-hauled stock with gangways throughout.

On refurbishment, many of these early EMU designs had gangway connections installed and compartment areas replaced with open saloons but, these changes aside, the BR fleet was highly successful and provided a reliable service with few teething problems. Another issue during overhaul was the removal of large amounts of blue asbestos from the fleet.

These first units were all supplied with dual voltage supply (6.25/25kV AC), the lower voltage being for use in station and tunnel/bridge areas with lower overhead line clearance, which was just 11 inches in places. The system was first trialled in Glasgow with the Class 303 'Blue Trains' with terrible results. Further research showed that safe clearance levels with 25kV could be lower than initially thought so, from 1962 onwards, the whole network was converted solely to the higher voltage. However, the 6.25kV supply soldiered on in some isolated areas, finally being removed from the sections from Leigh to Shoeburyness, and East Ham to Fenchurch Street, in 1989.

The Class 302s (AM2s) were introduced in 1958 on the London, Tilbury and Southend Railway and were based on the standard Mk.1 bodyshell. The 112 four-car units remained in service until 1999, most being withdrawn in the early 1990s and the remaining 30 refurbished sets being replaced by Classes 310, 312 and 317. Two driving trailers passed into preservation and are preserved at the Mangapps Railway Museum. Unit 212 is seen on a Liverpool Street to Witham service in the 1970s. (Andy Flowers Collection)

First Generation EMUs AC

TOPS Class	Builder	Design Code	No. of Carriages	Consist	Introduced	Withdrawn	Sets Built	Power Output	Max. Speed
(Allocated Class 301)	Metropolitan-Cammell	AM1	3	DMSO TS DTS	1952	1966	4	860hp	60mph
302	BR Doncaster/York	AM2	4	BDTS MBS TC DTS	1959	1999	112	768hp	75mph
303	Pressed Steel	AM3	3	BDTS MBS DTS	1959	2002	91	828hp	75mph
304	BR Wolverton	AM4	4	BDTS MBS TC DTBS	1960	1996	45	828hp	75mph
305/1	BR York	AM5	3	BDTS MBS DTS	1960	1995	55	800hp	75mph
305/2	BR Doncaster/York	AM5	4	BDTS MBS TC DTS	1960	2002	19	800hp	75mph
306	Metro-Cammell/BRCW	AM6	3	DMSO TBSO DTS	1949	1981	92	840hp	75mph
307	BR Eastleigh	AM7	4	DTBS MS TC DTS	1956	1993	32	700hp	75mph
308/1	BR York	AM8	4	BDTS MBS TC DTS	1961	2001	53	800hp	75mph
308/2	BR York	AM8	4	BDTS MLV TC DTS	1961	1983	5	800hp	75mph
308/3	BR York	AM8	3	BDTS MBS DTS	1961	1988	3	800hp	75mph
308/4	BR York	AM8	4	BDTS MBS TC DTS	1971	1992	4	1,128hp	100mph
309/1	BR York	AM9	4	DMBS TS TC BDTS	1961	1994	4	1,128hp	100mph
309/2	BR York	AM9	4	BDTC MBS TG DTC	1961	2000	8	1,128hp	100mph
309/3	BR York	AM9	4	BDTC MBS TS DTC	1961	2000	7	1,128hp	100mph
309/4	BR York	AM9	4	DMBS TS TC BDTS	1961	2000	4	1,128hp	100mph
310	BR Derby	AM10	4	BDTS MBS TS BDTC	1965	2002	50	1,080hp	75mph
311	Cravens	AM11	3	DTS MBS BDTS	1967	1990	19	828hp	75mph
312	BREL York	N/A	4	BDTS MBS TS DTC	1975	2004	49	1,080hp	75/90mph

Strathclyde PTE-liveried 303003 stands at Whifflet on 4 April 2000 on a Glasgow Central to Dalmuir service. The Class 303s, built by Pressed Steel, were introduced in 1960 for use on Glasgow suburban services and quickly became known as the 'Blue Trains' because of their distinctive livery. The sets, originally classified as AM3s, were finally withdrawn from service in 2002. 91 of the three-car units were built in total with one now preserved, this being a hybrid set formed from 303023 and 303032 and based at the Bo'ness and Kinneil Railway.

The Class 304s were part of BR's 1959 family of EMUs with many physical similarities to the other 25kV AC types, the Class 305s and 308s, and also the 1200V DC Class 504s. 45 of the four-car AM4 sets were built by BR at Wolverton for local services over the freshly electrified southern half of the West Coast Main Line in the 1960s. The fleet was refurbished in the early 1980s and reduced to three-car sets at the same time. Examples lasted in service until 1996 but no vehicles were preserved. 304027 stands at Coventry on 15 February 1988 forming a stopping service to Wolverhampton.

On 10 May 1998, 305519 arrives at Edinburgh Waverley on a service from North Berwick. The Class 305s were built in two batches with 52 '305/1s' (three-car sets) turned out from BR York and 19 '305/2s' (four-car sets) from Doncaster. The units, originally classified as AM5s, ran in service from 1959 to 2002. Initially used primarily in East Anglia, some sets later moved to the Manchester area while the last survivors saw out their last years in Scotland, based at Glasgow Shields and working local services between North Berwick and Edinburgh with some trains running through to Glasgow. No Class 305 vehicles were saved for preservation.

92 of the LNER-designed three-car Class 306s (originally designated as AM6s) were built by Metro-Cammell and BRCW and were introduced in 1949. Originally running off a 1500V DC overhead supply, the units were rebuilt to receive 25kV AC in the early 1960s. The fleet remained in service on Great Eastern metals until 1981. On 7 May 2002, sole survivor 306017 stands at Wickford on a special service to Southend Victoria, a number of additional workings being operated in connection with a Great Eastern steam weekend event. The unit was specially retained by BR throughout the 1980s and early 1990s for such special events before passing to the control of First Great Eastern, where it continued to be cared for at Ilford depot. The set is now part of the National Collection and is based at Shildon.

308163 arrives at Keighley on 31 July 1999 on the 12.01 Skipton to Bradford Foster Square. The Class 308s, built by BR at York, were introduced in 1961 for Liverpool to Shenfield and Southend services. 33 four-car Class 308/0s and five three-car Class 308/1s (with a central luggage car for use on Tilbury Line services) were built. Some Class 308s saw use in the West Midlands following the cross-city line electrification in 1993–94, prior to the introduction of the Class 323s into service. Electrification of the commuter lines north of Leeds saw a number of the class head north for services to Skipton, Ilkley and Bradford Foster Square in 1994–95. The units were replaced by Class 333s from 1999 with some of the Anglian sets remaining in service up to the new millennium.

Class 309 309617 stands at Manchester Piccadilly on 15 March 2000 after arrival on a service from Birmingham New Street. The '309s' were originally introduced for Clacton services, gaining the universal nickname of 'Clactons'. 23 of the units were built by BR at York and the fleet was in service from 1962 to 2000. Regional Railways North West had reactivated seven of the sets, stored at Blackpool at the time, and went on to use them on services between Birmingham International, Liverpool, Crewe and Manchester with some Manchester-Euston trains also featuring the luxury high speed EMUs.

After being replaced on their original West Coast Main Line duties by Class 323s in 2000, the Class 310s gravitated towards East Ham depot for use by the London, Tilbury and Southend operator LTS Rail. 310109 stands at Fenchurch Street with the officially organised farewell to the class; it is working the 15.10 to Shoeburyness on 17 November 2001. This was one of the 13 sets reduced to three cars in the 1990s and renumbered 3101101-113. The units were replaced on LTS metals by the new Class 357s.

The Class 311s, originally designated as AM11s, were built by Cravens of Sheffield in 1967. 19 of the three-car units, of a very similar design to the earlier Class 303s, were introduced following the extension of the Glasgow electrified network and were intended for services to Gourock and Wemyss Bay. In practice, they operated a wide variety of services over the Glasgow system alongside the Class 303s, although they were withdrawn en masse in 1990 in favour of the newer Class 318s. 311108 stands at Paisley Gilmour Street in December 1982. (Andy Flowers Collection)

312717 arrives at Manningtree on a terminating train from Harwich in February 2000. 49 of the four-car Class 312s were built by BREL at York between 1975 and 1978 and they remained in service until 2004. On introduction, they were used on Great Northern services from King's Cross to Royston, out of Liverpool Street and on some West Midlands semi-fast services to Liverpool Lime Street. Later, some units were used on London, Tilbury and Southend services. Two cars from 312792 were preserved and are now based at the Colne Valley Railway.

M59404M stands at Butterley, Midland Railway Centre, in the late 1980s after its transfer from the Dinting Railway Museum. Only the severed end of this vehicle now remains after the rest of the three-car unit was scrapped at Booth's Rotherham in 1995. Eight of the 'Hadfield' units were built for BR by Metro-Cammell and the Birmingham Railway Carriage and Wagon Company and they remained in service between 1954 and 1984 when the last remnants of the former Woodhead 1500V DC electrified network were converted to 25kV AC operation. (Andy Flowers Collection)

Chapter 4

First Generation Third-Rail DC EMUs

T he Southern Railway and its pre-grouping predecessors had favoured low voltage third-rail DC supply for its EMU fleets, a policy that applies right up to modern times. However, the most recent deliveries of EMUs to the former Southern Railway electrified zone are dual supply, or have been built with the option to include pantograph supply at a later date, leaving open the possibility of transferring them elsewhere in the country in the future.

Before World War Two, most of the EMUs operated on the Southern Railway area were formed from converted former locomotive-hauled coaching stock previously operated by the Southern's precursors, the London Brighton and South Coast Railway (LBSCR), South Eastern and Chatham Railway (SECR) and the London and South Western Railway (LSWR). The Southern Railway had inherited a wide range of different unit types from its pre-grouping precursors. The new company adopted a system of unit classification, comprising numbers and letters, the first number indicating the number of cars followed by a three letter code, for example 4-SUB for four-car suburban units.

The various unit types were often notoriously difficult to tell apart to the uninitiated, with the numbering system also disarmingly complex and confusing, adding further to the difficulties for the casual enthusiast. A programme of standardisation was gradually introduced by the Southern Region with larger and less diverse fleets of common types, a process that continued into the privatisation era.

BR designated the 1930s Southern Railway-built 2-BIL EMUs as TOPS Class 401 with the units used on semi-fast trains on the lines to Eastbourne, Portsmouth and Reading. 2111 is seen at an unidentified location in the late 1960s, after being repainted into BR corporate blue livery. The Class 401s, built at Eastleigh between 1935 and 1938, remained in service until 1971 with one set preserved, 2090 (cars 10656 and 12123) being owned by the National Railway Museum. (Andy Flowers Collection)

First Generation EMUs DC

Class	Builder	Type Code	No. of Carriages	Consist	Introduced	Withdrawn	Sets Built	Power Car Output	Max. Speed
405/1	Various/SR Eastleigh	4SUB	4	MBSO TS TSO MBSO	1941	1969	30	1,100hp	75mph
405/2	BR Eastleigh	4SUB	4	MBSO TS TSO MBSO	1957	1983	185	1,000hp	75mph
410	BR Eastleigh	4BEP	4	DMBS TC TRB DMBS	1957	2005	22	1,000hp	90mph
411	BR Eastleigh	4CEP	4	DMBS TC TS DMBS	1955	2005	110	1,000hp	90mph
412	BR Eastleigh	4BEP	4	DMBS TC TRB DMBS	1957	2005	10	1,000hp	90mph
414	BR Eastleigh	2HAP	2	DMBS DTC	1956	1995	42	500hp	70mph
415	BR Eastleigh	4EPB	4	MBSO TS TSO MBSO	1951	1995	335	1,000hp	75/90mph
416	BR Eastleigh	2EPB	2	DMBS DTS	1953	1995	112	500hp	75mph
418	BR Eastleigh	2SAP	2	DMBS DTS	1957	1983	32	500hp	75mph
419	BR Eastleigh	1MLV	1	MLV	1959	2004	10	500hp	90mph
420/422	BR York	4BIG	4	DTC MBS TRBS DTC	1964	2005	28	1,000hp	90mph
421	BR/BREL York	4CIG	4	DTC MBS TS DTC	1964	2010	38	1,000hp	90mph
423	BR/BREL York	4VEP	4	DTC MBS TS DTC	1957	2005	194	1,000hp	90mph
427	BR York	4VEG	4	DTC MBS TS DTC	1978	1984	12	1,000hp	90mph
430/432	BR York	4REP	4	MSO TRB TBF MSO	1966	1992	15	3,200hp	90mph
483	Metro-Cammell/BR Eastleigh	N/A	2	DMSO DMSO	1938 and 1989	2020	9	670hp	45mph
485	Metropolitan Cammell	4VEC	4	MBSO TSO DTSO MBSO	1967	1992	6	960hp	45mph
486	Metropolitan Cammell	3TIS	3	MBSO TSO MBSO	1967	1992	5	480hp	45mph
487	English Electric	N/A	2	DMBS TS	1940	1993	36	380hp	35mph
491	BR York	4TC	4	DTSO TF TBS DTSO	1966	1989	34	N/A	90mph
501	BR Eastleigh	N/A	3	DMBS TS DTBS	1957	1985	57	740hp	60mph
503	Metropolitan Cammell/BRCW	N/A	3	DMBS TS DTS	1938	1985	43	540hp	70mph
504	BR Wolverton	N/A	2	DMBS DTS	1959	1991	26	564hp	70mph
506	Metro-Cammell/BRCW	N/A	3	DMBS TS DTS	1954	1984	8	740hp	75mph

An undated view of 2-BIL EMU 1811 at West Croydon, though the presence of the BR totem station sign and the plain livery and styling of the unit indicate that this shot was taken some time in the 1950s. (Andy Flowers Collection)

The Southern Railway designated their long-distance EMUs working from Victoria to Kent as 2 HALs in the late 1930s. Any units that lasted into the BR TOPS era were designated as Class 402. Set 2692 arrives at Brighton with a stopping service from Ore in a very dated scene from the late 1960s. Of note are the trainspotters enjoying the arrivals from the ramp at the end of the platform. (Andy Flowers Collection)

The Southern Railway designated its luxury five-car London-Brighton Pullman EMUs as 5-BEL, these being allocated Class 403 in BR ownership. They were more commonly referred to as Brighton Belle units, taking their name from the Pullman service they operated. The units ran in service from 1932 to 1972 and a number of the individual vehicles have made it into preservation. Set 3053 stands at London Victoria on a Brighton service. (Andy Flowers Collection)

The Southern Railway allocated the designation 4-COR to one of the types of EMUs working the Waterloo to Portsmouth line, with those surviving into BR ownership gaining the TOPS allocation of Class 404. The last units survived in service with BR up until 1972. Set 3109 departs Ore with a train for Brighton via Eastbourne in the mid-1960s. (Andy Flowers Collection)

Southern Railway Maunsell-designed DMBTO vehicle 11179 from former express EMU 4-COR (later Class 404) 3131 is seen on display at the National Railway Museum. The vehicle has now been moved to the NRM's site at Shildon. (Andy Flowers Collection)

On 11 September 2020, DMBTO 8143 from 4-SUB 'Torpedo' EMU 1293 (later 4308) stands in the Great Hall at the National Railway Museum, flanked by GWR railcar No.4 and LMS Stanier 2-6-4T 2500. The designation SUB covered a wide range of different EMU types used on inner suburban services in the London area. Withdrawn in 1962, this unit would have been classified as 405/1 if it had survived into the BR TOPS era.

Class 405 4-SUB 4732, together with 2-BIL 2090, pause at Basingstoke on 27 September 1987 with a special working as part of the Basingstoke Rail Show. The EMU, formed of vehicles DMBTO 12795, TT 10239, TTO 12354 and DMBTO 12796, was retained by BR after withdrawal for special workings such as this. It is preserved and is currently held by Locomotive Storage Ltd at Margate. (Andy Flowers Collection)

A pair of Class 411 4-CEPs led by 1578 arrive at Clapham Junction on 4 April 2002 with a service from London Waterloo to Poole. The 4-CEPs were built by BR at Eastleigh Works between 1956 and 1963 to replace steam and diesel haulage of longer distance service on the newly electrified main lines in Kent. After privatisation, the fleet's use expanded westwards, being used by South West Trains, Connex South Central and Connex South Eastern. They remained in service between 1956 and 2005, the longest serving of BR's first generation third-rail EMU designs. A number of former CEP vehicles have been preserved at several locations around the country.

The Class 413 (4-CAP for Coastway) units were created from 1982 onwards by BR by the coupling together of 58 pairs of Brighton-based Class 414 2-HAP units. The sets were later transferred to the Eastern Division and the fleet was withdrawn by 1995, with no vehicles preserved. On 25 June 1987, 4-CAP 3205 departs from Sittingbourne on the 12.40 Ramsgate to London Victoria. (Andy Flowers Collection)

Class 415/1 (4-EPB) 5001 at Guildford on 3 July 1993 on a special working. This was the first of the type built, entering service on Waterloo to Guildford services in February 1952. The unit had been repainted into green livery in 1991 for use on special workings before its final withdrawal in 1994. The Southern-designed 4-EPBs were produced between 1951 and 1957 by BR at Eastleigh using reconditioned underframes and after the withdrawal of the Class 405 4-SUBs, they became the most numerous of the Southern Region EMUs with 213 sets built. The 4-EPBs were replaced in 1995 by second generation EMUs of Classes 465 and 466.

Class 415/4 (4-EPB) 5458 stands at London Bridge on an inner suburban Network SouthEast service on 11 January 1994. This sub-class was refurbished, renumbered 4-EPB and 'face-lifted' at Eastleigh Works from 1980 onwards. This unit was withdrawn in April 1994 and cut-up at Margam three weeks later. (Andy Flowers Collection)

BR built ten single car Class 419 Motor Luggage Vans (MLVs) at Eastleigh Works between 1951 and 1961, mostly to add extra luggage capacity on boat trains from London Victoria to Dover and Folkestone. After being originally numbered 68001 to 68010, the units gained the set numbers of 9001-10 under TOPS. One unusual feature was battery power, with the onboard batteries topped up from the third-rail supply, enabling around 20 minutes of running over unelectrified lines. The end of the Dover boat trains in 1992 saw the fleet pass into departmental use before withdrawal, although eight of the units have survived into preservation. 68003 (9003) departs London Victoria empty to Stewarts Lane depot in the early 1980s. (Andy Flowers Collection)

Class 421 4-CIG 1907 is seen between Three Bridges and Gatwick Airport on 3 April 2001 on a stopping service from London Victoria. The 4-CIGs have a complex numbering history, starting life numbered 7301 to 7438, then a variety of different systems before the final 19XX series. Built by BR/BREL at York in two batches and introduced in 1964 and 1970, the four-car units were the first of the third-rail designs specifically introduced for replacement of main line hauled stock and were initially used on the important Brighton Main Line. The second batch was produced for Portsmouth Line services.

The Class 422 4-BIG units were similar to the standard Class 421 4-CIGs but with a buffet car instead of one of the trailers. In line with the complexity of the Southern Region numbering system, the sets were initially classified under TOPS as Class 431/2 in 1972, then Class 420/2 in 1975, then 422/2 in 1983. In the unfamiliar location of the Great Central Railway, 4-BIG 7059 is propelled in push-pull mode on the 11.00 from Loughborough to Leicester North by resident Class 33/1 33116. After some metal theft at the railway, the set went on to be sold to RVEL Derby and some vehicles went on to form part of a Network Rail ultrasonic test train.

Class 423/9 (4-VOP) 3908 passes Clapham Junction on 9 January 2003 on an inner suburban working from London Victoria. Connex had 19 of its Class 423s modified in 1998–99 for use on inner suburban high capacity services. The units, renumbered as 4-VOPs 3901-19, had compartments, toilets and first-class areas removed to increase capacity by creating open plan interiors. The 4-VOPs were gradually replaced as Class 377s were introduced early in the 21st century. Set 3905 is preserved at the East Kent Railway.

Class 423/9 (4-VOP) 3903 approaches Gatwick on a stopping service on 4 April 2002. The converted 4-VOP sets were renumbered 3901 to 3919, further complicating the numbering system for the first generation Southern Region slam-door EMU fleet. The 4-VOPs remained in service with Southern until August 2005, being some of the last Mk.1-bodied stock still in regular use on the UK's rail network.

Left: The Southern Region Class 438s (4-TCs) were unpowered trailer stock that was fully compatible with most of the Southern Region's third-rail EMU fleet. Converted from existing Mk.1 coaches at York Works between 1966 and 1967, 34 sets were introduced with one spare DTSO. The units were mostly deployed between London Waterloo and Weymouth and in later years were also used as hauled stock with Class 50s on Waterloo-Salisbury services. The units remained in service until 1989 and a number of sets and several vehicles have been preserved. Set 417 is used by London Underground on services such as the 'Steam on the Met'. In the early 1980s, 8028 heads a Waterloo-Bournemouth working past Beaulieu Road in the New Forest.

Below: On 8 November 1970, an unidentified Class 501 stands at Watford Junction with a train for Euston, as identified by the B1 headcode. 57 of the three-car Class 501s were built in 1955–56 and remained in service until replaced by Class 313s in 1985. The LCGB (Croydon Branch) had chartered a 4-COR unit for a railtour around London, bringing the unusual sight on the next platform of set 3135. The DC lines from Euston had been converted from fourth-rail to third-rail operation only a few months earlier, allowing the 4-COR to travel over a wide range of new track for the type. (Andy Flowers Collection)

501150 pauses at Finchley Road on 19 August 1983, the B4 headcode indicating that this is a Broad Street to Richmond service. The Class 501s worked between Euston, Broad Street, Watford and Richmond, together with the Croxley Green branch. (Andy Flowers Collection)

The Class 503s or AM3s were introduced initially on the Merseyrail network by the LMS in 1938 with a second batch built under British Railways in 1956. The fleet was replaced by the Class 507s and 508s in 1985 with one set going on to be preserved at the Electric Railway Museum in Coventry and now moved to the Locomotive Storage Ltd warehouse at Margate. Car M28673 leads a six-coach formation into Birkenhead Central on a Merseyrail service to Liverpool Central, taken in the late 1970s. (Andy Flowers Collection)

Class 504 M77165 and M56444 are pictured at Manchester Victoria in September 1992. The two-car sets ran on the Manchester to Bury line's unique 1200V DC side contact third-rail system. The class consisted of the first BR EMUs with the new 1959-style cab as also used on the Class 304s, 305s and 308s. 26 of the units were built at BR Wolverton in 1959 and saw service until 1991 and the introduction of the Manchester Metro to Bury. (Andy Flowers Collection)

Chapter 5

First Generation DMUs

O n the formation of British Railways in 1948, the new nationalised body inherited only 37 DMUs; these being the 35 remaining GWR railcars and two of the NER's Armstrong Whitworths. The general post-war lack of diesel fuel and a plentiful supply of manpower meant there was little incentive to replace the steam locomotive fleet with new modern traction, and it was not until a committee report in 1952 that recommendations were made for wholesale dieselisation and the trial and introduction of lightweight diesel railcars.

The first DMU orders for Derby Works in 1952 coincided roughly with the end of fuel rationing, with anticipated use in West Yorkshire and Cumbria. The so-called Derby Lightweights utilised all steel open brake second stock, built around 1926, coupled with Paxman 450hp underfloor engines. After a successful trial run from Marylebone to Beaconsfield and return on 29 April 1954, the units went on to see successful service and led to the wholesale introduction of similar DMUs from the late 1950s onwards.

A DMU service was introduced between Leeds and Bradford on 14 June 1954 with services starting in Cumbria later in the year. The success of these early designs led to a recommendation in the British Transport Commission's 1955 report (The Modernisation Plan) for the introduction of up to 4,600 diesel railcars in a three-year construction programme, with many orders placed for the new stock in the same year.

The rush to build a large fleet, using whichever manufacturers were available, led to some unwelcome variations, including five different control systems, preventing large-scale multiple working between classes. The five types were: Red Triangle – Derby-built cars and later Bedford Line Class 127s; Yellow Diamond – Derby Lightweight and Metro-Cammell; White Circle – Swindon-built InterCity stock; Orange Star – Derby-built Rolls Royce engined sets; and Blue Square – all other DMU types, this covering 3,206 of the 3,810 DMU cars produced.

Fortuitously for the manufacturers and fans of DMUs, the end of much of the large-scale DMU production was timed well, just before the Beeching Plan with the closure of many of the branch lines for which the new units had been produced. The building programme for the new units was curtailed by the cuts and only 4,171 of the planned 4,600 vehicles were built, this including the Southern DEMUs, four-wheel light railcars and the Blue Pullmans.

Despite the downturn in overall track and passenger usage, the introduction of DMUs had been a huge success, the new stock delivering massive cost savings and an availability of around 86%. The travelling public were reported to be less keen on the new trains however, with numerous complaints about seating, ride quality and heating.

The British Railways Derby Lightweights were the first of the first generation DMUs built for fleet service, being constructed at Derby Works between 1954 and 1955 and consisting of 12 power-twin two-car units, 84 power-trailer two-car units and a quartet of four-car sets. Two single-car units were also built. A two-car Derby Lightweight set approaches Manchester Piccadilly in 1959. (Andy Flowers Collection)

First Generation DMUs

Class	Builder	Type	No. of Carriages	Consist	Introduced	Withdrawn	Sets Built	Power Car Output	Max. Speed
100	Gloucester RCW	LD	2	DMBS	1957	1988	40	300hp	70mph
101	Metro-Cammell	LD	2/3/4	DMBS DMC DTC TBS TC TS	1956	2003	Up to 270	150hp	70mph
103	Park Royal	LD	2	DMBS DTCL	1957	1983	20	300hp	70mph
104	BRCW	LD	2	DMBS DMC DTC TBS TC TS DHBS DHC	1957	1993	97	300hp	70mph
105	Cravens	LD	2/3	DMBS DMC DTC	1956	1988	Up to 142	300hp	70mph
107	BR Derby	LD	3	DMBS DMS DTC	1960	1991	25	300hp	70mph
108	BR Derby	LD	2/3/4	DMBS DMC DTC TBS TS	1958	1993	Up to 152	300hp	70mph
109	D Wickham and Co	LD	2	DMBS DTCL	1957	1971	5	300hp	70mph
110	BRCW	LD	2/3	DMBC DMC TS	1961	1991	30	360hp	70mph
111	Metro-Cammell	LD	2/3	DMBS DMC DHBS DHC	1957	1989	23	360hp	70mph
112/113	Cravens	LD	2	DMBS DMCL	1960	1969	50	576hp	70mph
114	BR Derby	LD	2	DMBS DTC	1956	2002	49	400hp	70mph
115	BR Derby	HD	4	DMBS TC TS	1960	1998	41	460hp	70mph
116	BR Derby	HD	3	DMBS DMS TS	1957	1990	Up to 103	300hp	70mph
117	Pressed Steel	HD	3	DMBS DMS TC	1959	2000	42	300hp	70mph
118	BRCW	HD	3	DMBS DMS TC	1960	1994	15	300hp	70mph
119	Gloucester RCW	CC	3	DMBC DMS TS	1958	1992	Up to 26	300hp	70mph
120	BR Swindon	CC	3	DMBS DMC DMBF TS	1957	1989	Up to 64	300hp	70mph
121	Pressed Steel	HD	1/2	DMBS DTS	1960	2017	16	300hp	70mph
122	Gloucester RCW	HD	1	DMBS	1958	1995	20	300hp	70mph
123	BR Swindon	CC	4	DMBS TC TS DMS	1963	1984	40	920hp	70mph
124	BR Swindon	CC	6	DMC MBS TS TF	1960	1984	8	460hp	70mph
125	BR Derby	LD	3	DMBS TS DMS	1959	1977	20	476hp	70mph
126	BR Swindon	CC	3	DMBS/DMS/TF/TC/TRBF	1959	1983	22	300hp	70mph
127	BR Derby	HD	4	DMBS TSL TS DMBS	1959	1993	30	476hp	70mph
127 (Parcels)	BR Derby	PCLS	2	DMNV DMPV	1985	1989	11	476hp	70mph
128	Gloucester RCW	PCLS	1	DMLV	1959	1990	10	460hp	70mph
129	Cravens	PCLS	1	DMLV	1958	1973	3	300hp	70mph

Left: The 20 two-car Class 100s were built by the Gloucester Railway Carriage and Wagon Company between 1956 and 1958, and remained in service until 1988 in the Glasgow, Birmingham and Manchester areas. On 24 October 1981, preserved DTC 56099 and DMBS 50341 approach Levisham on the North Yorkshire Moors Railway, the photo taken from the footplate of Austerity 0-6-0T *Antwerp*. The unit was later sold to the Swanage Railway then transferred on to the West Somerset and scrapped in 1991. (Andy Flowers Collection)

Below: The Class 101s were the most numerous (with 760 individual vehicles built) and most successful of BR's first generation DMUs and lasted in service from 1956 to 2003. They saw service nationwide but by the turn of the century their use was restricted to one operator, First North Western, and like the end of steam, the final first generation DMUs saw their last days in use in Lancashire and the North West. In their final year of operation along the North Wales Coast, 101676 passes Penmaenmawr on 8 May 2000 working the 12.00 Holyhead–Llandudno.

101684 leaves Glasgow Central on 4 April 2000 on a service for Whifflet. Scotrail inherited 11 Class 101 sets upon privatisation in 1997, and the class lasted in Scotland until the year 2000, right up to the introduction of the new deliveries of Class 170 Turbostars and the cascade of available Class 156s. The Glasgow-based 101s worked services from Central to Barrhead, Paisley Canal, East Kilbride, and Whifflet as well as Motherwell to Cumbernauld. Some of the Scottish 101s were transferred to the Manchester area, with many retaining their Strathclyde Transport livery.

Park Royal Class 103 set 50414 and 56168 at Blue Anchor on the West Somerset Railway in the mid-1980s. This set was unfortunately scrapped in 1993 after the railway's whole DMU fleet was withdrawn in 1989 following the discovery of asbestos in some vehicles. 20 of the two-car sets were built in 1956/57, being initially based around Chester and Watford (for the St Albans and Belmont branches), then Walsall before moving to the Western Region. The whole class was withdrawn by 1983. (Andy Flowers Collection)

On 5 June 1992, hybrid set L730 is seen between Twyford and Maidenhead on a London Paddington to Reading stopping service. This unit has coincidentally been preserved with Class 104 DMBS 53455 now based at the East Lancashire Railway and Class 108 DMCL 51571 now found on the Kent and East Sussex Railway. The Class 104s did not last long on Thames Valley services, being moved there from the Gospel Oak-Barking line at the beginning of 1992 to work alongside the indigenous Class 117s before they were replaced by Class 165/1s the following year. (Andy Flowers Collection)

The Class 105s were built by Cravens of Sheffield between 1956 and 1959 and remained in service until 1988. In total, 302 vehicles were ordered with units formed into a mixture of two and three car sets for use mainly on the Eastern Region with some use in Scotland and a few duties around Birmingham for those based at Tyseley. A preserved Class 105 DMU comprising DMBS 51485 and DTCL 56121 waits at Bishops Lydeard on a service to Minehead in the mid-1990s. The set is now based at the East Lancashire Railway and is operational. (Andy Flowers Collection)

On 3 July 2007, the Keighley and Worth Valley Railway's resident Class 108, formed of DMCL 51565 and DMBS 50928, stands at Keighley with a service for Oxenhope. The set had been bought by Bradford Metropolitan Council in 1992 for preservation on their local heritage line to assist the railway in providing out of season and off-peak services to help alleviate car traffic congestion along the Worth Valley. More than 50 individual Class 108 vehicles have been preserved on heritage railways, which is testament to the reliability and popularity of the design.

A fleet of five two-car units was built by D Wickham and Co in 1957 and remained in service until 1971 after they were deemed non-standard. Classified as Class 109, a set is seen at the unlikely location of the closed station of Warsop (on the line from Shirebrook to Thoresby Colliery) with a number of elderly and clearly easily pleased passengers on a special working from Lincoln on the 3 May 1975. This unit, formed of vehicles DMBS DB975005 and DTCL DB975006, served as the Eastern Region's General Manager's saloon after withdrawal from regular service and was regularly chartered for special workings such as this. (Andy Flowers Collection)

On 4 April 1981, a Calder Valley set with vehicles 51841, 59704 and 52067 approaches Preston with a service for Blackpool North. The Class 110s were built by the Birmingham Railway Carriage and Wagon Company for services in Lancashire and Yorkshire and were essentially an uprated Class 104. 30 of the three-car sets were built between 1961 and 1962, although many were reduced to two-car formation in the early 1980s. The type remained in service until 1991 with one two-car set preserved at the Lakeside and Haverthwaite Railway and one three-car set at the East Lancashire Railway. (Andy Flowers Collection)

Class 115 DMBS 51887 stands at Minehead on the West Somerset Railway in the summer of 2003 on a train from Bishops Lydeard. The non-authentic carmine and cream livery lasted only a few years. 41 of the high density four-car units were introduced in 1960 for commuter services out of London Marylebone to Banbury, High Wycombe and Aylesbury. They lasted in service until 1994 with 15 of the vehicles passing into preservation. (Andy Flowers Collection)

On 31 May 2008, Class 116 DMBS 51131 stands at Shackerstone on a service for Shenton, on the Battlefield Line, accompanied by Class 122 'Bubble Car' M55005. The Class 116s were built at Derby between 1957 and 1961 for nationwide use and remained in service until 1990. 108 of the two or three car sets were constructed (108 DMBS, 108 DMS and 94 TC) and they saw use on the Birmingham Cross-City Line, together with Class 101s, before replacement on completion of electrification of the route in 1993. Other sets saw use in the south west of Scotland, the Cardiff Valleys and out of Liverpool Street and King's Cross.

Preserved Class 117 DMU 117420 (DMS 51400) is seen at Leeming Bar on the Wensleydale Railway on 11 June 2017. This vehicle moved to the line in May 2008 and is often paired with Class 121 55032 for services to Redmire. The '117s' were a Pressed Steel licence-built version of the BR Class 116s, being constructed between 1959 and 1961 for heavily loaded suburban commuter services, largely out of Paddington and Reading.

The BRCW Class 118s were another licence-built version of the Class 116s. In service from 1960 to 1994, the 45 cars were generally formed into 15 three-car sets. For most of their lives, they worked on the Western Region though, in later years, they were all reallocated to Tyseley. On 23 July 1980, set P468 formed of vehicles 51325, 59471 and 51310 passes Winterbourne on the 18.15 Paddington to Bristol. (Andy Flowers Collection)

Above: A Class 120 DMU comprising vehicles 53722, 59523 (a Class 101 trailer) and 53672 is pictured at Llandanwg, near Harlech, in the mid-1980s on a service from Pwllheli to Shrewsbury. 64 of the three-car cross-country 'Swindon' units were built by BR at the eponymously named works between 1957 and 1960 with the units based nationwide including at Cambridge, Chester, Derby, Edinburgh Haymarket and Reading. The 'Sprinterisation' of regional services in the 1980s saw the fleet withdrawn by 1989. One vehicle, TSLRB 59276, has been preserved at the Great Central Railway. (Andy Flowers Collection)

Right: Class 121 121020 arrives at Princes Risborough on a service from Aylesbury on 1 March 2003. Chiltern Railways had reintroduced Class 121 'Bubble Cars' on the Aylesbury shuttle in 2003, with 121020 repainted into Chiltern blue livery and fitted with central door locking via electromagnets in the door footwells. Chiltern went on to introduce a second set in 2011, 121034. The units were withdrawn from service in May 2017 when more Class 165s became available and the cost of keeping the first generation DMUs in traffic became uneconomic.

Class 122 'Bubble Car' M55005 passes Market Bosworth (Battlefield Line) on 9 September 2020 working the 11.00 Shackerstone to Shenton, it being coupled with Class 116 DMBS 51131. 20 of the Class 122s were built by Gloucester RC&W in 1958 with nine single-cabbed trailers added to the fleet later. A number of the units went on to see departmental use after ending their careers on passenger duties.

The Class 123s were built by BR at Swindon Works in 1963, the last of the early DMUs to be assembled there. Ten four-car sets were produced, initially intended for Portsmouth to Bristol and Cardiff services. However, they were put straight to use on many longer distance cross-country services between Derby, Swansea, Birmingham, Crewe and Bristol. From 1970, they were concentrated on Paddington to Newbury and Oxford services before being transferred to the Eastern Region in 1977. In January 1980, set 710 stands at Doncaster on a Hull to Manchester via Sheffield and the Hope Valley service; DMBS E52090 is the lead vehicle pictured. Class 31/4s and hauled coaching stock took over these services in May 1984 with the Class 123s and similar Class 124s withdrawn en masse around the same time. Set 710 was withdrawn from Hull Botanic Gardens on 19 September 1984. (Andy Flowers Collection)

The Class 124 DMUs, commonly referred to as Trans-Pennine units, were built by BR at Swindon in 1960 and remained in service until 1984. Eight six-car sets were constructed with three spare cars. The sets were based at Hull and Leeds Neville Hill for use on Hull and York to Liverpool services. A Trans-Pennine set is seen passing Chaloners Whin Junction on 20 April 1976 working the 15.15 York to Liverpool Lime Street. (Barrie Watkins/Andy Flowers Collection)

30 four-car high density DMUs of Class 127 were built at BR Derby in 1959 for use on St Pancras commuter services, mostly to Bedford. The sets were withdrawn after completion of the Bedford electrification out of St Pancras and the corresponding introduction of the Class 317 EMUs. The Loco Club of Great Britain ran a farewell tour for the 'Bed-Pan' units from St Pancras to the Buckingham Railway Centre on 12 March 1983 using vehicles 51592, 59615, 59645 and 51618, seen here at Quainton Road. (Andy Flowers Collection)

Ten single-car units, designated Class 128 under TOPS, were built by the Gloucester Railway Carriage and Wagon Company for parcels traffic, these being based at Coldham Lane (Cambridge), Reading and Tyseley. They saw service from 1959 to 1990 and none of the units passed into preservation. An unidentified member of the class is seen at Leicester in the 1990s. (Andy Flowers Collection)

Chapter 6

Diesel-Electric Multiple Units

The Southern Region of British Railways adopted a different approach to the replacement of steam power with EMUs favoured for most lines and DEMUs for the unelectrified branches and minor routes. The 1951 Bowes Report included provision for some DEMUs to replace steam in the Hampshire area, although the need to improve services on the Hastings line saw the first diesels introduced there instead with electrification being prioritised for the Dover main line at the time. The 'Hastings' units were built to the restricted gauge required on the route because of the narrow tunnels between Tunbridge Wells and Hastings.

The first DEMUs were based on a design supplied to the Egyptian State Railways in 1947, though appearance-wise, the new stock owed more to the styling of traditional Southern third-rail EMUs, particularly the 2-HAPs. The power units installed were English Electric 4SRKT rated at 500hp, these giving the units their distinctive sound and leading to the nickname for the group (Classes 201 to 207) of 'Thumpers'.

The new units were introduced into squadron service between Charing Cross and Hastings from 1957 and they were an immediate success. The later three-car sets for Hampshire lines included a trailer and an uprated 600hp power unit, which was installed to give a better power-to-weight ratio and to ensure that timings were kept. However, the higher power rating of the power unit led to some issues in terms of maintenance and reliability. 26 more three-car sets were ordered in 1962 to take over Reading to Portsmouth services along with Oxted and East Sussex lines, ranging from Victoria to East Grinstead, Tunbridge Wells and Brighton via Uckfield.

The findings of the Beeching Report again curtailed further construction with many of the DEMU routes coming under threat of closure. Three of the original 'Hastings' sets were withdrawn in 1964 with their power cars reformed into hybrid 'Tadpole' sets, so named because of their varied body widths, and were used on the line between Redhill and Reading via Tonbridge. The 'Thumper' family worked widely

'Hastings' unit 1001 stands at Charing Cross on 5 February 2002 on the 17.12 to Hastings. The celebrity preserved unit was hired to work services over the line for a few weeks at the beginning of 2002 to provide cover for unavailable 'Electrostar' EMUs being introduced at the time. The presence of smoke alarms under the roof meant that the DEMU needed to be parked at the platform end – diesel traction not being generally used at Charing Cross. 1001 was the first of the Southern DEMUs but this particular incarnation consists of a number of vehicles from different sets.

across the Southern Region, even over electrified routes, and were also occasionally used on longer distance services, including Class 205s on Portsmouth to Bristol and Weston-Super-Mare services.

Franchise commitments to withdraw all Mk.1-bodied rolling stock saw the last surviving DEMUs dispensed with by the deadline of the end of 2004. Thanks to the largesse of leasing company Porterbrook, many members of Class 205 were donated to preserved lines and the Hastings Class 201 set 1001 has gone on to attain celebrity status in preservation with a wide range of main line tours operated over much of the British rail network.

DEMUs

Class	Builder	Type	No. of Carriages	Consist	Introduced	Withdrawn	Sets Built	Power Car Output	Max. Speed
201	BR Eastleigh/ Ashford	LD	6	DMBS TSO TSO TFK TSO DMBS	1957	1986	7	500hp	90mph
202	BR Eastleigh/ Ashford	LD	6	DMBS TSO TSO TFK TSO DMBS	1958	1987	9	500hp	90mph
203	BR Eastleigh/ Ashford	LD	6	DMBS TSO TBU TFK TSO DMBS	1958	1990	7	500hp	90mph
204	BR Eastleigh	LD	2 (3 from 1979)	DMBS TC / +DTS	1957/1979	1987	8 (4 rebuilt 205s)	600hp	75mph
205	BR Eastleigh	LD	2/3	DMBS TC / +DTS	1957	2004	34	600hp	75mph
206	BR Eastleigh	LD	3	DMBS TC DTS	1964	1982	6	600hp	75mph
207	BR Eastleigh	LD	3	DMBS TC DTS	1962	2004	19	600hp	75mph
210	BR Derby	HD	3/4	DMBS TSO (+/- TCO) DTS	1982	1987	2	1,125/ 1,140hp	90mph

The numbering history of the Class 204s, in typical Southern Region fashion, is complex. The original '204s' were two-car versions of the Class 205s, classified as 2H and numbered 1119–1122. In 1979, after adding an extra trailer taken from Class 205s, most of the fleet were reclassified as Class 205s too. Newly formed units, made up by adding driving trailers from Class 206s and the remnants of the Class 205s from which the centre trailers had been donated, were then reclassified as Class 204s (or 3Ts) and renumbered 1401–1404. Class 204 DEMU 1404 arrives at Reading on a service from Portsmouth in 1982. The unit was withdrawn along with the rest of the fleet in 1987. One original Class 204 vehicle has been preserved, DTCL 60820, reformed into Class 205 set 205008 and based on the Lavender Line. (Andy Flowers Collection)

The Class 205 (3H) DEMUs were used by BR between 1957 and 2004 and were employed on a wide variety of services over the unelectrified lines of the Southern Region. After electrification of the East Grinstead Line in 1987, the remaining units were concentrated on the Ashford to Hastings, and London to Uckfield lines. On privatisation, the fleet passed to Connex South Central, then Govia (Southern), which ordered Class 171s from Bombardier to replace the remaining DEMUs as part of its franchise commitments. On 13 May 2002, 205012 stands at Ashford with a service for Hastings, one of the last holdouts for the 'Thumpers'.

Class 205 DEMU 205032 waits at Basingstoke on the evening of 15 February 1988 on a service for Salisbury. This unit was withdrawn in 2004 and has been preserved, currently in operational status, on the Dartmoor Railway.

207005 leaves Overton on a Basingstoke to Salisbury service in February 1988. This unit was later named *Brighton Royal Pavilion*, refurbished and renumbered as 207102, then later 207202. The 19 three-car Class 207 DEMUs (3D) served with BR and later Connex South Central and Southern from 1962 to 2004. Three full sets have been preserved including 207017 at the Spa Valley Railway, 207202 at the East Lancashire Railway and 207203 at the Swindon and Cricklade Railway.

Originally envisaged as a replacement for BR's ageing Mk.1 DEMU fleet, the Class 210s were built at Derby in 1982. Only two units were produced for evaluation, four-car 210001 and three-car 210002, the latter being pictured at Reading West on 22 November 1986 on a train for Newbury. No follow-on orders for the units were placed but one vehicle is preserved, DMSO 67300 at the East Kent Railway. (Andy Flowers Collection)

Chapter 7

Second Generation EMUs

B R began the process of replacing its first generation EMU classes, both AC and DC, in the early 1970s with the Southern Region leading the way with the introduction of the PEP Class 445/446 prototypes. The new units featured automatic sliding doors and a number of other technological advances. They were tested extensively on the Southern and their success saw BR order a number of new designs for use nationwide, starting with what became known as 1972 High Density Stock, namely Classes 313, 314, 315, 507 and 508. Soon after these, the Class 455s began to be delivered and replacement of the original Mk.1-dervied EMUs on the Southern Region really began to accelerate.

The need for sliding doors, both for safety and to speed up loading and unloading times, had been foreseen with some of the earlier BR EMU types, particularly the Class 303s and 311s. The newer units were often based on the Mk.2-hauled coaching stock bodyshells or, in some cases for longer

313104 arrives at Euston in February 2001 on a suburban stopping service. Built at York Works, the dual-voltage Class 313s can operate from third-rail or overhead supply. Introduced in 1976, 20 of the original 64-strong fleet of three-car units remain in service. Formerly used by Silverlink and West Anglia Great Northern, the class is now concentrated on the south coast. The remaining units are used by Southern on east and west coastway services from Brighton and some services to Portsmouth, Lewes, Hove and Seaford.

distance services, the later Mk.3s, such as the Class 442s. Other areas of improvement on the newer stock included driver-controlled automatic coupling and uncoupling with the Tightlock coupler becoming the new standard for a time. This was combined with Westcode type braking, which was an electro-pneumatic system now fully electrically controlled with a single main reservoir pipe and a three-step brake.

The new trains also featured air suspension to increase ride quality and reduce track wear. Traction motor numbers were increased and they were moved from a central position to the outer vehicles. Rheostatic braking became more practical as technology advanced and newer lighter traction motors were introduced. The new units also saw the end of a separate luggage area and guard's compartment, the guard now generally sitting in the rear cab with controls situated there for door opening and passenger announcements.

The second generation EMUs with their ease of use and servicing, though often very basic passenger accommodation, heralded a new type of more cost-conscious rolling stock, a policy that has continued to this day.

Second Generation EMUs AC

Class	Builder	Type	No. of Carriages	Consist	Introduced	Withdrawn	Sets Built	Power Car Output	Max. Speed
313	BRCW	HD	3	DMS TC BDMS	1960	n/a	15	300hp	70mph
314	BREL York	HD	3	DMS TS DMS	1979	n/a	16	880hp	75mph
315	BREL York	HD	4	DMS TS TS DMS	1980	n/a	61	880hp	75mph
317	BREL Derby/ York	HD	4	DTS MS MS DTS	1981	n/a	71	1,328hp	100mph
318	BREL York	HD	3	DTS MS DTS	1986	n/a	21	1,328hp	100mph
320	BREL York	HD	3	DTS MS DTS	1990	n/a	22	1,438hp	90/100mph
321	BREL York	HD	4	DTC TS PMS DTS	1988	n/a	117	1,438hp	100mph
322	BREL York	HD	4	DTS TS MS DTS	1990	n/a	5	1,438hp	100mph
325	ABB Derby	Parcels	4	DTPMV MPMV TPMV DTPMV	1995	n/a	16	1,438hp	100mph

314205 waits at Glasgow Central in February 2001 on an evening Cathcart Circle service. The Class 314s, built in 1979 by BR at York, were used on Glasgow area inner suburban services until 2019. 16 of the three-car units were constructed and have now been replaced by Class 318s and 320s following the arrival of the newer Class 380s and 385s. 314209 has been retained as a test-bed for hydrogen-powered operation.

314214 leaves Glasgow Central on a Cathcart Circle train on 30 March 2000. The Class 314s were essentially a higher capacity version of the Class 313s, which was achieved by removing seating and increasing the standing area around the doors. The units were well suited to the Strathclyde PTE orange and black livery.

315839 awaits departure from London Liverpool Street on 2 October 2020 on 2W10, the 14.50 to Shenfield. The Class 315s were built at BREL York between 1980 and 1981 as the last variant of the standard 1972 (PEP) suburban EMU design. 61 of the four-car sets were built for use on Great Eastern and West Anglian Great Northern services. Since 2015, they have been operated by Abellio Greater Anglia, London Overground and, currently, TfL Rail. The fleet was fully replaced on London Overground services by Class 710s during 2020.

On 15 June 2001, 317661 leaves Potters Bar on a Peterborough to King's Cross service. Built between 1985 and 1987, the unit is from the second batch of Class 317s that featured a slightly revised front end and were used on Great Northern services between King's Cross, Cambridge and Peterborough, later expanding to Ely and King's Lynn following the extension of electrification. The Class 318s in the Glasgow area are a closely related design, being three-car sets rather than four-cars.

318256 arrives at Glasgow Central on 30 March 2000 on a Cathcart Circle working. The Class 318s were introduced in 1986 as the Glasgow suburban electrification was extended to Ayr and Ardrossan. 21 three-car sets were built at BREL York between 1985 and 1986 and they have been refurbished twice in their history, firstly by Hunslet Barclay, Kilmarnock, between 2005 and 2007, and most recently by Wabtec in Doncaster between 2013 and 2017. The units are the oldest EMUs in regular use in Scotland.

319216 approaches Gatwick Airport on a Bedford to Brighton service on 11 April 2001. These highly versatile units are capable of operating on a 25kV AC overhead supply or 750V DC third rail, with 86 of the four-car units being built by BREL at York. In service from 1987, initially largely on Thameslink duties, 47 of the sets are still in service and they have widened their sphere of operation to include use on the recently electrified lines in the north west with a smaller number operated by London Northwestern on the West Coast Main Line and the Abbey Line from Watford Junction to St Albans Abbey. Some of the fleet are currently being rebuilt as hybrid-powered Class 769s.

The Class 320 EMUs were built by BREL at York for the electrified suburban network around Glasgow in 1990 with 22 three-car sets (Class 320/3s) built and 12 later converted from Class 321/4s (Class 320/4s) – the '321s' effectively being a four-car version of the same unit. The fleet has recently been refurbished and should remain in service for a number of years to come. On the 4 April 2000, 320305 arrives at Hyndland on a Milngavie to Motherwell service via Glasgow Central.

321409 approaches Tile Hill on 20 May 2000 on the 08.25 Birmingham New Street to London Euston semi-fast service via Northampton. The Class 321s were built by BREL at York in three batches between 1998 and 1991, these being designated Class 321/3, 321/4 and 321/9. Initially, the fleet saw use on stopping services over the southern half of the West Coast Main Line with some work out of King's Cross and later with Northern out of Leeds. 117 sets were outshopped with 12 later converted to Class 320s. All of the remaining Class 321 fleet are now operating with Greater Anglia.

On 15 February 2005, 321424 leaves Rugby on a London Euston to Birmingham New Street semi-fast West Coast Main Line service. Silverlink County (owned by National Express) was the franchise holder for local and inter-urban passenger services between March 1997 and November 2007, with Silverlink Metro (London suburban) services then taken over by London Overground and the longer distance services towards the West Midlands by London Midland.

323215 passes Berkswell on a Coventry to Wolverhampton stopping service in June 2001. The Class 323s were the last major rolling stock order for Hunslet of Leeds with 43 of the three-car sets built between 1992 and 1993. After entering traffic on suburban services in the Manchester and West Midlands areas, the fleet is still fully in use today with West Midlands Railway and Northern. The 26 sets in use in the West Midlands are due to be transferred to Northern in 2021 with a life-extension refurbishment being carried out.

The Class 325s are dedicated postal EMUs built by ABB at Derby between 1995 and 1996. 16 of the four-car sets were produced and are of a similar design to the Class 319s with dual voltage capacity as built, but fitted with similar cabs to the 'Networker' family of EMUs. Based at Crewe Electric TMD, the units are used on postal traffic over the West Coast Main Line with one train also run over the East Coast from Willesden to Low Fell, near Newcastle. On 15 April 2020, 325016 passes Cathiron, north of Rugby, on an empty working, this being 5A91, the 11.20 Crewe Electric to Willesden Princess Royal Distribution Centre.

The Class 334 EMUs were built by Alstom at its Washwood Heath plant, Birmingham, and are operated by Abellio ScotRail on its suburban services in the Glasgow area. 40 of the three-car sets were built between 1999 and 2000 and the fleet was refurbished between 2012 and 2014. On 4 March 2000, 34032 leaves Glasgow Central on a service to Gourock.

365538 heads for London King's Cross from Potters Bar in April 2001 on a service from Peterborough. The Class 365 'Networker Express' units were built to operate services in Kent and on the Great Northern route out of King's Cross. They were the last EMUs built at York Works before its closure. 41 four-car sets were introduced in 1996 and 21 of the units are still running today with many in store at Crewe. They have been largely relegated to peak-hour duties only following the introduction of the newer Class 387s and 700s.

Second Generation EMUs DC

TOPS Class	Builder	Code	No. of Carriages	Consist	Name	Introduced	Withdrawn	Sets Built	Power Output	Max. Speed
424	Adtranz		1	DSO	Networker Classic Prototype	1997	2012	1	n/a	100mph
442	BREL Derby	5-WES	5	DTFL DTS TS TS MBRSM	Wessex Express ("Plastic Pigs")	1988	n/a	24	1,610hp	100mph
444	Siemens	5-DES	5	DMCO TSRMB TSO TSO DMSO	Desiro	2004	n/a	45	2,680hp	100mph
445	BREL	4-PEP	4	DMSO MSO MSO DMSO		1973	1980	2	1,600hp	75mph
446	BREL	2-PEP	2	DMSO DMSO		1971	1980	1	800hp	75mph
450	Siemens	4-DES	4	DMSO TCO TSO DMSO	Desiro	2003	n/a	127	2,682hp	100mph
455	BREL York		4	DTSO MSO TSO DTSO		1982	n/a	137	1,000hp	75mph
456	BREL York		2	DMSO DTSO		1991	n/a	24	500hp	75mph
457	BREL/RTC Derby		4	DMSO TSO TSO DMSO	Networker Prototype	1989	1991	1	1,140hp	90mph
458	Alstom	5-JOP	5	DMCO PTSO TSO DMCO/DMSO TSOLx2 MSO DMSO	Juniper	2000	n/a	30	2,172hp	75/ 100mph
460	Alstom	8-GAT	8	DMFL TFO TCO MSO MSO TSO MS DMSO	Gatwick Juniper	2000	2012	8	3,620hp	100mph
465	BREL/Metro-Cammell/ABB		4	DMSO TSO TSOL DMSO	Networker	1992	n/a	147	1,608hp	75mph
466	Metro-Cammell		2	DMSO DTOS	Networker	1993	n/a	43	804hp	75mph
507	BREL York		2	BDMSO TSO DMSO		1978	n/a	33	880hp	75mph
508	BREL York	4-PER	2	DMSO TSO BDMSO		1979	n/a	43	880hp	75mph

'Wessex Electric' Class 442 (5-WES) 2417 passes Clapham Junction on 4 April 2002 on a London Waterloo to Southampton service. 24 of the five-car sets, with bodyshells based on the standard BR Mk.3 coach, were built at Derby Litchurch Lane between 1987 and 1989 for use on the newly electrified main line to Weymouth. They have been given life-extension refurbishment work twice, once by Southern in 2008, which used the sets on Gatwick and Brighton services, and later by South Western Railway in 2017–18 for use on the Waterloo to Portsmouth route.

The Siemens Class 444 EMUs belong to the 'Desiro' family and were introduced in 2004 for use on the London Waterloo to Portsmouth and Weymouth routes. A pair of units, led by 444045, pass through Clapham Junction on 9 October 2020 working 1W69, the 14.00 Waterloo to Weymouth service.

450015 pauses at Basingstoke on 15 June 2006 on a London Waterloo to Southampton service. The Class 450s, built between 2002 and 2006 and introduced from 2003, were built at Krefeld, Germany, and are the most numerous members of the 'Desiro' family of Siemens units, which also includes Classes 185, 350, 360, 380 and 444. 127 of the four-car units were built and today they comprise a large proportion of the outer-suburban and longer distance rolling stock on South Western Railway. The units occasionally stand in for the slightly more spacious Class 444s on Portsmouth services.

On 9 January 2003, Class 455/7 5709 passes Clapham Junction on a service from Windsor and Eton Riverside to London Waterloo. 505 separate Class 455 carriages were built by BREL York between 1982 and 1985 and, together with 43 cars inherited from Class 508 units, 137 four-car EMUs were formed for suburban commuter duties on the South Central and South Western areas of BR's Southern Region. The Class 455/7s are distinguishable by their different cab front with a more curved roof and also feature a TS car taken from a donor Class 508.

The three batches of Class 455 are all four-car sets but there are some noticeable physical differences between the sub-classes, the Class 455/8s being distinguished by a squarer front end cab design. 5843 passes Clapham Junction on 9 January 2003 on an inner suburban service. There have been a number of upgrades to the heavily used fleet, though the class is likely to be gradually withdrawn over the next few years as more of the new Class 701 'Aventra' units are introduced.

The 20 Class 455/9 four-car inner suburban sets built in 1985 are distinguishable from the Class 455/7s, which share the same rounded cab design, by having the same roof profile for each vehicle. On 9 October 2020, 5914 passes Clapham Junction on a service from Waterloo paired with a Class 456 unit.

On 9 January 2003, two of South West Trains' Class 458 (4-JOP) units, led by 8012, pass Clapham Junction on a service from London Waterloo to Reading. A number of technical issues delayed the 30-strong fleet's introduction into service until 2000 and continuing issues saw the entire class returned to leasing company Porterbrook once the Class 450s had entered service. The fleet was returned to traffic with South West Trains in 2006-07 after modifications in order to allow the Class 442s to move to Southern and they remain in service today.

The eight-car Class 460s built for Gatwick Express duties from London Victoria were part of the Alstom 'Juniper' family, which included Classes 334 and 458. The sets had a delayed introduction into service between 1999 and 2005 and were not a great success, being withdrawn in 2012. Eight sets were built at Washwood Heath and only saw use on the Gatwick services. The sets were subsequently rebuilt at great cost as Class 458/5s with four driving vehicles kept as spares donors then scrapped at Booth's, Rotherham. 460006 passes Clapham Junction on 9 January 2003 on a train for Gatwick Airport.

460004 arrives at Gatwick Airport on 3 June 2002. The Stewarts Lane-based Class 460s were also termed 8-GAT and capable of 100mph operation, the sets gaining the nickname of 'Darth Vaders' due to their distinctive cab shape. The class was gradually removed from service from the end of December 2010 and replaced by refurbished Class 442 'Wessex' units. The final Class 460 sets were taken off lease in September 2012.

On 12 July 2005, 465163 and 465019 arrive at Beckenham Junction on a London to Sevenoaks service. 50 of the four-car Class 465/0s were built by BREL York between 1991 and 1993 with 47 more or less identical Class 465/1s following in 1993–94. Metro-Cammell contributed another 50 Class 465/2s in 1991–93, these having a number of design differences. The 'Networkers' were introduced in October 1992 and were operated initially by Network SouthEast, then in turn by Connex South Eastern up to 2003, South Eastern Trains to 2006 and then up to the present day by the current franchise holder Southeastern.

On 12 July 2005, York-built units 465019 and 465163 stand at Beckenham Junction with a London to Sevenoaks service. The leading set is carrying the interim Connex livery with vinyls applied over part of the Network SouthEast colours, while it also has modified front fairings in an effort to stop 'train-surfing'.

The Class 483s, originally built as 1938 London Transport tube stock, were refurbished at Eastleigh between 1989 and 1992 in order to replace the Class 485s and 486s on the Isle of Wight. The vintage units were finally withdrawn in December 2020 ahead of newly converted Class 484s taking over from early 2021. 483008 arrives at Ryde Esplanade on 3 September 2020 with 2U42, the 15.18 Shanklin to Ryde Pier Head.

The Class 485s together with the 3-TIS Class 486s were former tube stock built in the 1920s and 1930s that was overhauled at London Transport's Acton Works for use on the newly electrified Ryde Pier Head to Shanklin (Isle of Wight) line, services commencing in 1967. The final units were withdrawn in 1992 and replaced by the Class 483s. 4-VEC 485045 in BR corporate blue livery arrives at Sandown in 1969. (Andy Flowers Collection)

The Class 489 GLVs were EMUs converted to be used in conjunction with Mk.2 conventional hauled stock and Class 73s in push-pull mode on London Victoria to Gatwick Airport services. 10 of the DMLVs were converted from Class 414/3 DMBS vehicles at BREL Eastleigh in 1983–84 and the sets operated between 1984 and 2005. The modified hauled stock was designated as Class 488. The GLVs and Class 488 stock were replaced on Gatwick Express services by Class 460 'Juniper' units. Network Rail bought four of the GLVs for departmental use as de-icing vehicles, and four others went on to be preserved at heritage lines. 9108 arrives at Gatwick Airport on the rear of a Class 73-hauled rake on 3 April 2001.

507028 arrives at Chester on a service from Birkenhead in February 2001. The Class 507s were the first of the PEP derived family of EMUs (Classes 313, 314, 315, 507 and 508) that could operate only on the 750V DC system and as such have worked only on the Merseyrail network, along with Class 508s. Still in use, 33 three-car sets were introduced in 1978 and are amongst the oldest EMUs in use in the UK but are due to be replaced from this year by the new Stadler-built Class 777s.

Class 508 508117 arrives at Hooton on a Chester to Liverpool service in the late 1980s. 43 of the three-car units were built by BREL at York between 1979 and 1980 to the 1972 BR standard EMU design. The fleet was introduced on suburban services out of London Waterloo in the early 1980s, later being reduced from four-car to three-car sets and transferred to the Merseyside area. The units have subsequently seen wide-ranging use, 12 of the sets were leased to Connex South Eastern in 1996 for use in Kent, and three were used by Silverlink from 2003 between Watford Junction and Euston. 27 of the sets in use with Merseyrail were refurbished between 2002 and 2004 at Eastleigh and 25 of them are still in use, although due to be replaced from this year. (Andy Flowers Collection)

Chapter 8

Second Generation DMUs

While the first generation DMUs and DEMUs brought in under the Modernisation Plan to replace steam traction on unelectrified branches and minor/secondary routes had been, by and large, highly successful, their large-scale introduction within a relatively short time period meant that they were becoming due for mass replacement by the late 1970s.

BR looked at a number of options for the replacement programme including the Class 210s to replace the Southern Region DEMUs. Other projects included the LEV prototypes and Class 140 as pioneers for new lightweight railcars for branch line duties and the Class 151s for urban and longer distance traffic. While the Class 210s proved to be reliable and comfortable units, their high costs saw BR look instead to conventional DMUs to replace the elderly Southern Region DEMUs.

The LEV prototypes proved that light railcars based on bus bodyshells could deliver a cheap and reliable service, making many low use branch lines economically viable, and led on to the development and introduction of the 'Pacer' and 'Skipper' classes of 141, 142, 143 and 144.

Passenger feedback from the light railcars led BR to look at more comfortable options for longer distance travel. After evaluating four prototypes, two Class 150s from BREL and two Class 151s from Metro-Cammell, the former won out and were developed into a new large 'Sprinter' fleet. This eventually totalled more than 1,000 vehicles and included Classes 153, 155,156 and 158. The 'Sprinters', in turn, promoted complaints from the travelling public compared to the previous trains (often locomotive-hauled coaching stock) but by this stage, the DMUs, with their benefits in terms of cost and ease of use, were firmly entrenched as the main form of motive power on the unelectrified railway.

140001 leaves Preston on 16 September 1981 on the 11.20 to Ormskirk. The Class 140 was a prototype DMU, the forerunner of the Class 141 and Class 142 'Pacer' units and was constructed largely using components shared within Leyland National road buses. The unit, built by BREL at Derby Litchurch Lane, saw service on trial across a wide area of the British Rail network between 1981 and 1986. 140001 was preserved from its own depot (Neville Hill) in 1995 and is now based at the Keith and Dufftown Railway. (Andy Flowers Collection)

Second Generation DMUs

Class	Builder	Type	No. of Carriages	Consist	Introduced	Withdrawn	Sets Built	Power Car Output	Max. Speed
LEV1	BR	HD	1	DM	1979	1987	1	200hp	75mph
139	Parry	HD	1	DM	2009	n/a	2	86hp	20mph
140	BREL	HD	2	DMS DMS	1981	1981	1	205hp	75mph
141	Leyland/BREL	HD	2	DMS DMS	1983	1997	20	205hp	75mph
142	Leyland/BREL	HD	2	DMS DMS	1985	2020	96	205/225hp	75mph
143	Alexander/ Barclay	HD	2	DMS DMS	1985	2020	25	205/225hp	75mph
144	Alexander/ BREL	HD	2/3	DMS DMS/ DMS MS DMS	1986	2020	23	205/225hp	75mph
150/0	BREL York	LD	3	DMS MS DMSL	1984	n/a	2	286hp	75mph
150/1	BREL York	LD	2	DMS DMSL	1985	n/a	50	286hp	75mph
150/2	BREL York	LD	2	DMS DMSL	1987	n/a	85	286hp	75mph
151	Metro-Cammell	LD	3	DMS MS DMS	1985	1989	2	855hp	75mph
153	Hunslet Barclay	HD	1	DMSL	1991	n/a	70	286hp	75mph
154 (ex-150)	BREL	LD	3	DMS MS DMSL	1987	2011	1	286hp	75mph
155	Leyland	LD	2	DMS DMSL	1987	n/a	35	286hp	75mph
155/1	Leyland	LD	2	DMS DMSL	1988	n/a	7	286hp	75mph
156	Metro-Cammell	LD	2	DMS DMSL	1987	n/a	114	286hp	75mph
158/0	BREL	LD	2/3	DMSL (+-MS) DMSL/DMC	1989	n/a	172	350/400hp	90mph
158/9	BREL	LD	2	DMS DMSL	1991	n/a	10	350/400hp	90mph

Class	Builder	Type	No. of Carriages	Consist	Introduced	Withdrawn	Sets Built	Power Car Output	Max. Speed
159/0	BREL	LD	3	DMSL MSL DMCL	1992	n/a	22	350/400hp	90mph
159/1	BREL Wabtec	LD	3	DMSL MSL DMCL	2007	n/a	8	350/400hp	90mph
165	BREL York	LD	2/3	DMCL (+-MS) DMSL	1990	n/a	76	350hp	75/90mph
166	BREL York	LD	3	DMCL MS DMCL	1993	n/a	21	350hp	90mph
168	Bombardier Derby	LD	4	DMSL MSL MSL DMSL	1998	n/a	19	422hp	100mph
170	Adtranz/ Bombardier Derby	LD	2/3	DMSL (+- MSL) DMCL	1998	n/a	122	422hp	100mph
171	Bombardier Derby	LD	2/4	DMSL (+- 2xMS) DMCL	2003	n/a	16	422hp	100mph
172	Bombardier Derby	LD	2/3	DMSL (+-MS) DMSL	2010	n/a	39	483hp	100mph
175/0	Alstom	LD	2	DMSL DMSL	1995	n/a	11	450hp	100mph
175/1	Alstom	LD	3	DMSL MSL DMSL	1999	n/a	16	450hp	100mph

141115 pauses at Knottingley in the late 1980s on a service to Leeds. The Class 141s were the first of the production fleets of the 'Pacer' family to be introduced in 1984 and they remained in service until 1997. 12 of the notoriously uncomfortable units were exported in 2001 to Iran, a country that had surely suffered enough already! The last of the UK fleet was withdrawn from departmental service in 2005. (Andy Flowers Collection)

On 14 November 2019, Class 142 142020 stands at York after arrival on a service from Harrogate. These 'Pacers' are now withdrawn from main line operations due to their non-compliance with disabled access regulations. At the end of their life, the Class 142s were split between the Northern and Transport for Wales franchises and should have been withdrawn during 2019 but gained a stay of execution in order to enable longer trains to run in connection with social distancing measures for the COVID-19 virus. The final Northern sets were withdrawn in December 2020 with the last Welsh examples following in 2021.

On 14 April 2003, 143609 leaves Ystrad Mynach leading a Class 142 on a Bargoed to Cardiff Bay service over the Rhymney Line. The Class 143s were introduced in 1985 for use in the north east before the fleet was transferred to Wales and the south west. 25 of the two-car sets were built by Hunslet-Barclay and Walter Alexander of Falkirk between 1985 and 1986. New disabled access legislation meant that the 'Pacers' needed to be withdrawn by 1 January 2020 but problems in replacing the sets (prior to the collapse in passenger numbers during the COVID-19 outbreak) saw an extension granted by the Department for Transport to enable the sets to stay in use until early 2021 in Wales.

A pair of Class 143 units led by 143605 stand at Cardiff Central on 2 July 2006 on a Treherbert to Cardiff Queen Street service. Both units are finished in Arriva Trains Wales livery, the franchise operator between 2003 and 2018. The company, unlike many other franchise holders, sensibly restricted the use of 'Pacer' units to shorter distance routes, mainly the Valley Lines to Rhymney, Treherbert, Merthyr Tydfil, Aberdare and Coryton.

Class 150/1 150105 leaves Stourbridge Junction on 1 June 2002 with a service to Leamington Spa via Snow Hill. The non-gangwayed Class 150/1s were generally two-car sets, although a third car could be added from a separated Class 150/2. Central Trains inherited 85 Class 150 cars from BR on privatisation in 1997 with the livery being Centro, which was a modified version of the standard 1990s Regional Railways colours for use in the West Midlands area. Three versions of the Class 150 were built by BREL at York between 1984 and 1987, totalling 137 units, with the Class 150/2s easily distinguishable by their cab gangway connections.

151002 stands at Derby on a service for Matlock in March 1986. Only two Class 151s were built by Metro-Cammell in 1985 as prototypes for the new 'Sprinter' fleet to be introduced by BR, the design losing out to the rival BREL Class 150/0s. After a few years of testing, the two units were withdrawn in 1989 and after spells of storage in various locations and under different ownerships, both units were scrapped at Crewe in 2004. (Andy Flowers Collection)

On 15 January 2017, 153365 waits at Nuneaton on the 22.14 to Coventry. The Class 153s are conversions of the original two-car Class 155 'Sprinters' into two single car units; 70 vehicles were created at the Kilmarnock workshops of Hunslet-Barclay in 1991–92 for secondary and branch use. The West Yorkshire Passenger Transport Executive retained its seven-strong fleet of unmodified Class 155s. West Midlands Trains had a fleet of eight Class 153s for use on the line between Leamington and Nuneaton via Coventry and also Bedford to Bletchley services, both now replaced by Class 172s and Class 230s respectively.

The Class 155s, which were originally termed 'Super Sprinters' along with the Class 156s, were built between 1987 and 1988 by Leyland Bus at Workington and included some parts shared with the company's buses. 35 of the original 42-strong fleet were later converted into single car Class 153s with only seven of the original build remaining. Allocated to Neville Hill depot in Leeds, the survivors are largely restricted to duties in Yorkshire for Northern, particularly from Hull to Scarborough and York. On 14 November 2019, 155344 stands at York awaiting its next turn of duty.

156464 arrives at Llandudno Junction on 8 May 2000 on a service from Llandudno to Crewe. Metro-Cammell built 114 two-car Class 156 sets for BR between 1987 and 1989 and all of the fleet remain in service today across much of the network. 156464 is seen sporting the Regional Railways North West livery but is now leased to First North Western. Class 156 operators had been reduced to just three by 2020, namely Abellio ScotRail, East Midlands Railway and Northern.

156483 waits at Newcastle on the evening of 15 November 2019 on a service to Carlisle. Northern inherited its Class 156 fleet from Arriva Trains Northern and First North Western in 2004 with the units continuing to see widespread use across the north of England.

Central Trains-liveried 158857 passes Lea Marston, between Kingsbury and Water Orton, on a Nottingham to Birmingham New Street service on 15 June 2002. The Class 158 fleet was built by BREL at its Derby Litchurch Lane Works between 1989 and 1992. 172 of the two or three-car sets were built for use across the BR network on higher-speed inter-regional work and core commuter services. All of the fleet are still in service today with operators including East Midlands Railway, Great Western Railway, Abellio ScotRail, Northern, South Western Railway and Transport for Wales. Central Trains subsequently relegated its '158' fleet to shorter-distance secondary duties including Derby to Matlock and Birmingham to Hereford when it took delivery of the new Class 170s from 1999 onwards.

East Midlands Trains 158770 passes Cossington (north of Leicester) on the Midland Main Line on 15 June 2012 working a Cambridge to Birmingham New Street service. East Midlands Trains, owned by the Stagecoach Group, operated the franchise between 2007 and 2019 and maintained a fleet of 26 Class 158s. These saw use over much of its network between Liverpool, Norwich, Crewe and Lincoln.

Above: 158872 stands at York on 2C45, the 20.11 to Leeds via Harrogate, on 27 November 2019. The franchise was previously operated as Northern Spirit, then Arriva Trains Northern and Northern Rail and, from 1 March 2020, the government-owned Northern. All of its Class 158s have been refurbished in recent years and they should remain in service for a few more years, despite the recent introduction of new CAF-built Class 195 units.

Left: Class 159/0 159017 passes Clapham Junction on 9 January 2003 on a service from London Waterloo to Salisbury. The Class 159s are part of the 'Sprinter' family and were built by BREL at Derby Litchurch Lane during 1992 before entering service the next year on West of England duties from Waterloo to Salisbury and Exeter. 22 three-car Class 159/0s were initially provided, these requiring modifications from new to fit first-class accommodation and retention toilet tanks as they were built to Class 158 specification. Under South West Trains, eight three-car Class 158s were acquired from TransPennine Express in 2007 and similarly upgraded to Class 159/1s.

Chapter 9

Third Generation EMUs

The development of new technology, particularly in the areas of solid state switching devices such as transistors and thyristors (semiconductor electronic switches) and other areas of electronic power control, have seen the third generation of EMUs become ever more complex. Dual supply has also become much more common with many types delivered with both third-rail 750V DC and 25kV AC capability. This has further enabled use on through services crossing London from north to south, including Thameslink services and trains from the West Coast Main Line passing on to the former Southern Region.

Starting with the Class 323s built by Hunslet in 1992, the latest generation of EMUs used on Britain's railways represent a step change in many areas, including reliability, acceleration and braking. New foreign-based suppliers, including Siemens, Hitachi and CAF, have introduced a wide variety of new multiple unit types and driven an increase in technological change on the network.

The next advances in EMU technology may feature active suspension, new types of regenerative braking, magnetic track braking, increased automation and active couplings. The future will undoubtedly involve the continuing, and no doubt increased, use of the electric multiple unit powering the majority of railway passenger services in Britain.

Third Generation EMUs DC

TOPS Class	Builder	No. of Carriages	Consist	Name	Introduced	Sets Built	Power Output	Max. Speed
700	Siemens	8/12	DMCO PTSO MSO TSOX2 MSO PTSO DMCO/ DMCO PTSO MSOX2 TSOX4 MSOX2 PTSO DMCO	Desiro City	2016	115	4,400/ 6,700hp	100mph
701	Bombardier	5/10	DMS PMS TS MS DMS/DMS PMS TSX4 TS PMS DMS	Aventra	2020	90	2,695/ 5,390hp	100mph
707	Siemens	5	DMSO TSO TSO PTSO DMSO	Desiro City	2017	30	1,600hp	100mph
710	Bombardier	4/5	DMSO MSO PMSO (+- MSO) DMSO	Aventra	2019	54	357hp	75mph
717	Siemens	6	DMSO TSO TSO MSO PTSO DMSO	Desiro City	2017	25	1,600hp	100mph

Third Generation EMUs AC/Hybrids

TOPS Class	Builder	No. of Carriages	Consist	Name	Introduced	Sets Built	Power Output	Max. Speed
323	Hunslet Leeds	3	DMSO TSOL DMSO	DMS TS DMS	1992	n/a	3,550hp	100mph
331/0	CAF	4	DMSO PTS DMSO	Civity	2019	31	4,700hp	100mph
331/1	CAF	4/5	DMSO PTS TS DMSO	Civity	2019	12	4,700hp	100mph
332	Siemens	4	DMFO TSO PTSO DMSO/DMFLO	n/a	1998	14	1,900hp	100mph
333	Siemens/CAF	4	DMSO PTSO TSO DMSO	n/a	2000	16	1,900hp	100mph
334	Alstom	5	DMSO PTSO DMSO	Juniper	2000	40	1,448hp	90mph
345	Bombardier	7/9	DMS PMS MS/2 TS MS/2 PMS DMS	Aventra	2017	70	6,700hp	90mph
350	Siemens	4	DMSO TCO PTSO DMSO	Desiro	2005	87	2,010hp	110mph
357	Adtranz/Bombardier	4	DMSO MSO PTSO DMSO	Electrostar	2000	74	2,000hp	100mph
360	Siemens	4/5	DMCO PTSO TSO DMCO	Desiro	2003	26	2,080hp	100mph
375	Bombardier	3/4	DMCO TSO/MSO (+-PTSO) DMCO	Electrostar	1999	112	2,012hp	100mph
376	Bombardier	5	DMSO MSO TSO MSO DMSO	Electrostar	2004	36	2,662hp	75mph
377	Bombardier	3/4	DMCO (+-MSO) TSO DMCO	Electrostar	2002	182	2,012hp	100mph
378	Bombardier	5	DMOS MOS PTOS MOS DMOS	Capitalstar	2009	57	3,200hp	75mph
379	Bombardier	4	DMCO MSO TSO DMCO	Electrostar	2011	30	2,012hp	100mph

TOPS Class	Builder	No. of Carriages	Consist	Name	Introduced	Sets Built	Power Output	Max. Speed
380	Siemens	3/4	DMSO PTSO (+-TSO) DMSO	Desiro	2010	38	1,341hp	100mph
385	Hitachi Rail	3/4	DMSO PTSO (+-TSO) DMSO	AT200	2018	75	2,010hp	100mph
387	Bombardier	4	DMSO PTSO TSO DMSO	Electrostar	2014	107	2,250hp	110mph
397	CAF	5	DMF PTS MS PTS DMS	Civity	2018	12	3,540hp	125mph
399	Vossloh	3	DMSO MSO DMSO	Tram-Train	2017	7	1,166hp	60mph
720	Bombardier	5/10	DMSO PMSO MSOX2 (TSO MSO PMSO MSOX2) DTSO	Aventra	2020	139	3,500/7,000hp	100mph
730	Bombardier	3/5	n/a	Aventra	2021?	81	n/a	90/110mph
745	Stadler	12	(DMF/S TS TS MS TS PTS)x2	FLIRT	2020	20	7,000hp	100mph
755	Stadler	3/4	DMSO (+-PTSO) PTSOW DMSO	FLIRT	2019	38	3,500hp	100mph
756	Stadler	3/4	n/a	FLIRT	2023?	24	n/a	n/a
769	Brush (rebuild)	4	DMSO/DMCO/DTSO MSL/MSO TSO DMSO/ DTSO	Flex	2021?	41	1,328hp	100mph
777	Stadler	4	DMS MS MS DMS	Metro	2021?	52	2,820hp	75mph
799	Quinton Rail Technology	4	DMSO MSO TSO DMSO	Hydroflex	2021?	1	1,328hp	100mph

The Class 230s are diesel-electric DMUs or battery EMUs, converted from London Underground D78 Stock, formerly used on the District Line of the London Underground. The units can also operate as hybrids with an intermediate car housing diesel generator sets. On 24 September 2020, 230002 stands outside the main VivaRail workshops at Long Marston. This set is the only multiple unit in the UK, at the time of writing, authorised to operate on the British network on battery power and is due to travel to the USA as a demonstrator for the new traction technology.

230008 runs through Stourbridge Junction on 29 September 2020 on a 10.32 Moreton-in-Marsh to Stourbridge Junction test run. The set was freshly outshopped by VivaRail at Long Marston and was being tested and run in for use by Transport for Wales on its Wrexham to Bidston services. The hybrid sets, outshopped in the new TfW white and red livery, are powered by two batteries on the driving cars and four diesel power unit sets in the centre car. They are due to enter service in mid-2021 once testing and driver training is completed.

331106 stands at Leeds station on 11 September 2020 on 2B25, the 17.22 stopping service to Doncaster. The Spanish CAF-built Class 331s are owned by Eversholt Rail Group and are leased to Northern for services between Leeds and Doncaster, and West Yorkshire routes operated by Class 333s. In the north west, they see use between Liverpool, Blackpool North, Manchester Airport and Crewe. As a regular visitor to Leeds since the 1970s, the rebuilt station is now barely recognisable from that of the steam and diesel era.

Above: On 9 October 2020, 332002 departs London Paddington on 1T21 the 14.25 Heathrow Express service to Heathrow Airport Terminal 5. In the adjoining Platform 8, an empty stock Heathrow Express service (3Z37, the 14.34 departure) is being worked by recently converted Class 387/1 387131. These modified 'Electrostars' replaced the Class 332s at the very end of 2020 with the latter then going for scrap. 14 of the four or five-car Class 332s were built in Zaragoza, Spain, by CAF and were owned by the British Airports Authority for the dedicated shuttle from Paddington to Heathrow.

Right: 333012 arrives at Keighley on 14 July 2001 on a service from Leeds to Ilkley. 16 of the four-car 100mph-capable Class 333s were built by Siemens and CAF between 2000 and 2001, being a development of the Class 332s. They are based at Neville Hill for use on Northern's electrified commuter lines to Bradford, Ilkley and Skipton. The entire fleet was refurbished between 2018 and 2020 and further refurbishments are planned, meaning that the units are likely to remain in service for the foreseeable future.

The Class 345 EMUs have been built by Bombardier for use on Crossrail (now named the Elizabeth Line) running from Reading and Heathrow Central to Shenfield and Abbey Wood via Paddington. 70 of the currently seven- or nine-coach sets were built at Derby between 2015 and 2019 (630 carriages in total) and they are maintained at Old Oak Common and Ilford. The new units were still being commissioned and entering service at the time of writing. On 20 August 2020, 345068 calls at Ealing Broadway on 9P56, the 11.52 Reading to Paddington service.

On 18 January 2013, Class 350/1 350127 stands at Coventry on a stopping service from London Euston via Northampton. Four sub-classes of the Siemens 'Desiro' Class 350s were supplied, these all being similar to the third-rail Class 450s. The Class 350/1s were introduced first with 30 of the four-car units built between 2004 and 2005 for use on semi-fast West Coast Main Line services. The sub-class has dual supply capability and some were leased to Southern in 2008-09 to cover for 'Electrostars' hired to First Capital Connect.

On 13 July 2005, 357013 stands at Barking on a service from Shoeburyness to London Fenchurch Street. The Class 357s were built at Derby Litchurch Lane by new owners Adtranz following the end of BREL. 74 of the four-car units were produced between 1999 and 2003, the initial sets entering service in 2000 as the first members of the 'Electrostar' family, which went on to include Classes 375, 376, 377, 378, 379 and 387. The units are classified as Class 357/0s (the original batch), 357/2 (the second batch) and 357/3 (those units converted in 2015–16 with 2+2 seating instead of 2+3).

The Class 360 EMUs were built by Siemens as part of the 'Desiro' family between 2002 and 2005, seeing use on outer suburban passenger duties with Greater Anglia and Heathrow Connect, the latter coming under the control of Transport for London in 2018. On 20 August 2020, 360205 arrives at Acton Main Line on 9P61, the 12.52 Heathrow Airport Terminal 5 to Paddington. The five Class 360/2s ended 2020 in store and probably facing sale overseas after being replaced by the Class 345s. Meanwhile, the 21 Class 360/1s used by Greater Anglia were in the process of being transferred to East Midlands Railway for use on the new electric services between St Pancras and Corby/Kettering.

On 13 July 2005, Class 375/8 375801 stands at Beckenham Junction on a service from Bromley South to London Victoria. The Class 375s are a member of the Bombardier 'Electrostar' family with 140 of the three- or four-car units built at Derby between 1999 and 2001. 28 of the sets were later converted to Class 377/3s with different couplings. The Class 375s have always been concentrated in the south-eastern area of what was BR's Southern Region, working out of London Victoria, Charing Cross and Cannon Street to locations in Kent. The class also took over duties on the Sheerness line from Class 466s at the end of 2019. There are four variants: 375/3 (three-car sets), 375/6 (four-car dual voltage sets), 375/7 and 375/8 (four-car DC-only sets) and 375/9 (high density units).

On 12 July 2005, 376011 approaches Lewisham on a Southeastern stopping service. The Class 376s are also 'Electrostars' with 36 five-car sets being introduced in 2004 with South Eastern Trains, these replacing Class 465 and Class 466s on London to Dartford and Orpington trains, together with the remaining Class 423 (4-VEP) slam-door units on faster Kent services. The '376s' have wider doors than other 'Electrostars', enabling faster loading and unloading on busy commuter routes. Provision was made when built for a pantograph to be added at a later date to enable overhead supply.

The Class 377s are the most numerous of the third generation EMUs built post privatisation, with 211 of the three-, four- or five-car units produced, together with 28 additional sets produced by converting Class 375/3s. On 24 July 2005, a pair of Class 377s led by 377160 approach Clapham Junction on a Southern service from London Victoria to Brighton. Sub-classes have been built as follows: 377/1 (third rail only), 377/2 (dual voltage for through services over the WCML), 377/3 (three-car sets converted from 375s), 377/4s (third rail only), 377/5 (dual voltage sets transferred from Thameslink to Southeastern), 377/6 (higher density sets) and 377/7 (five-car dual voltage sets).

377209 stands at Watford Junction on 13 July 2005. The Class 377/2s were procured to operate the Southern services between Milton Keynes Central and Brighton utilising their dual voltage supply capabilities, work that was subsequently shared with the longer Class 377/7s following their arrival. The Class 377/2s are also used to cover for other sub-classes on services to Brighton and other Southern routes. 15 of the type were built and introduced between 2002 and 2003.

A total of 57 of the five-car Class 378 'Capitalstar' units were built by Bombardier between 2008 and 2010, the first entering service in July 2009. The type has been designed exclusively for use on the London Overground network and is based on the Class 376s but with longitudinal seating and much greater standing space for high capacity inner suburban use. The first sets were built as three-car, then later extended to four- and then five-car vehicles. There are two sub-classes, the 20 Class 378/1s used on the East London and South London lines are third rail only, while the 37 dual voltage Class 378/2s are used on the North, West, East and South London lines. On 20 August 2020, 378135 pauses at Acton Central on 2N65, the 13.40 Richmond to Stratford.

Another 'Electrostar' variant, the 30 four-car Class 379s were built between 2010 and 2011 to replace Class 317s on services between London Liverpool Street, Cambridge, King's Lynn and Stansted Airport, and also to expand capacity. The sets are allocated to Ilford and have been operated by Greater Anglia since September 2017. On 2 October 2020, the new order of EMUs on the Great Eastern was on show as 379001 stands at Liverpool Street on 2H38, the 14.58 to Cambridge North, next to Class 710/1 710112 on 2U50, the 15.00 to Enfield Town.

380102 is seen at Edinburgh Waverley on 15 February 2019 on a service to North Berwick. The Siemens Class 380s belong to the 'Desiro' family and are operated by Abellio ScotRail on Edinburgh and Glasgow suburban services. 22 of the three-car Class 380/0s and 16 of the four-car Class 380/1s were built between 2009 and 2011 at Siemens' Krefeld plant in Germany, entering service at the end of 2010 and based at Glasgow Shields. (Andy Flowers Collection)

107 of the four-car Class 387 EMUs were built by Bombardier as part of the 'Electrostar' design and they are essentially a dual-supply version of the earlier Class 379s. They first saw use in 2014 with Thameslink. There are three sub-classes: 74 Class 387/1s in service with Great Northern, Great Western and Heathrow Express, 27 Class 387/2s with Southern/Gatwick Express and six Class 387/3s with c2c. On 20 August 2020, 387149 arrives at Reading on 2N52, the 15.57 London Paddington to Didcot Parkway. With electrification deferred as far as Oxford, the Class 387-operated semi-fast services from Paddington have been cut back to Didcot with a diesel service onwards.

The 750V DC two-car third-rail Class 484s are being constructed by VivaRail at the Quinton Rail Technology Centre, Long Marston, these being converted from ex-District Line D78 Stock. Originally built by Metro-Cammell between 1978 and 1981, five of the units are due to be delivered to replace the Class 483s on Isle of Wight services. On 24 September 2020, 484001 enters the final stage of assembly and fitting out at VivaRail's site. The Island Line's Class 483 stock was withdrawn at the end of 2020 with the route then closed until the end of March 2021 for upgrading before the introduction of the Class 484s.

700050 stands at London King's Cross on 5 January 2019 after arrival on a stopping service from Peterborough. Part of the Siemens 'Desiro City' family of EMUs, the Class 700s were built between 2014 and 2018 for the Thameslink lines with 60 eight-car and 55 twelve-car sets allocated to Hornsey and Three Bridges depots. These entered service in June 2016 and replaced the previously used Class 319s on the cross-London routes and some Class 365s on Great Northern services. The units can operate on third-rail and overhead supply.

A pair of Class 707 'Desiro City' units with 707020 at the rear head out of Clapham Junction on 9 October 2020 while working 2S36, the 12.33 Weybridge to London Waterloo. 30 of the five-car units were built by Siemens between 2015 and 2018 and introduced from 2017 onwards for South Western Railway services out of London Waterloo to Windsor and Eton Riverside, Weybridge via Hounslow, Kingston, Woking and Guildford. The fleet will be replaced on its current duties as more of the new Class 701s are introduced, enabling the 707s to transfer to Southeastern.

On 2 October 2020, Class 710/1 710112 stands at Liverpool Street on 2U50 the 15.00 to Enfield Town. The class was introduced into service in May 2019 on the Gospel Oak to Barking line. Class 710/1s (the AC only variant) are still being introduced on Great Eastern (Lea Valley) lines from Liverpool Street to Enfield, Cheshunt and Chingford after their debut in March 2020. The planned fleet of 54 four-car Class 710 'Aventras' has now been completed by Bombardier at its Derby Litchurch Lane plant for use on the London Overground network and will enable the withdrawal of Classes 315 and 317 along with the redeployment of the newer Class 378s.

The dual-supply Class 710/2s have been ordered by Transport for London to expand capacity on its overground system and replace some of the remaining second-generation EMUs in use on suburban passenger services around the capital. The 710s are the latest in a long line of different EMU types to be used on the DC Lines between London Euston and Watford Junction, taking over from Class 378s. Class 710/2 710264 stands at Euston on 2 October 2020 on 2D70 the 12.58 to Watford Junction.

On 9 October 2020, 717022 stands at Moorgate on 2V59 the 11.32 to Welwyn Garden City. Many of the London Overground inner-city stations closely resemble the style and layout of their Tube equivalents, often, as here, having their origins with the original Underground operators, in this case the Northern City Line. The Class 717s, another member of the 'Desiro City' family, are leased by Govia Thameslink Railway and work from Moorgate over the Hertford loop and on to Welwyn. Built at Krefeld, Germany, between 2018 and 2019, the 25-strong fleet of six-car units differs from the similar Class 700s by the provision of cab front emergency doors for tunnel evacuation purposes.

The Bombardier Class 720 'Aventra' EMUs are currently under construction at Derby Litchurch Lane. 133 five-car Class 720/5 units are being built for Greater Anglia and six Class 720/6 10-car sets for c2c. Both fleets are designed for semi-fast services, being similar to the Class 345s but with a higher maximum speed of 100mph and more spacious saloon areas. The newly built units are being tested on the West Coast Main Line between their temporary base at Wolverton and Crewe via Nuneaton. On 11 August 2020, 720539 heads south back to Wolverton on 5Q28, the 13.51 Rugby-Wolverton via Crewe test run.

Chapter 10

Third Generation DMUs

P rivatisation of British Rail in the mid-1990s saw a hiatus in rolling stock orders, and when purchasing of new trains finally began again, the new owners were Rolling Stock Leasing Companies (ROSCOs) rather than the train operators. The new franchise holders continued the cost-cutting move away from locomotives and coaches for many of their intercity and regional services, preferring the more cost-effective DMU option, even on longer cross-country routes.

The years since privatisation have seen an expansion in new stock orders, with most of the units supplied being delivered from overseas manufacturers, like Siemens and Bombardier, although often assembled in the UK. As with the third generation series of EMUs, the development of new technology has seen a number of big advances in diesel multiple units in terms of automation, control, access and features. New concepts such as controlled emission toilets have greatly improved the onboard and trackside environment with air conditioning, power points and passenger information screens all adding to the experience for the commuter and leisure traveller.

The next few years will more than likely see the continuing decarbonisation of the railways and, short of full electrification, alternative traction packages will be introduced for unelectrified branches, such as battery power or hydrogen. In either event, the days of the DMU are limited. In the next few decades, the DMUs in use on preserved lines may seem as nostalgic to today's enthusiasts as steam locomotives remain to many of today's older generation.

Third Generation DMUs

Class	Builder	Type	No. of Carriages	Consist	Introduced	Withdrawn	Sets Built	Power Car Output	Max. Speed
185	Siemens	LD	3	DMOSB MOSL DMOCLW	2006	N/A	51	1,500hp	100mph
195	CAF	LD	2/3	DMSO (+-MS) DMSOL	2019	N/A	58	1,046hp	100mph
196	CAF	LD	2/4	DMSL (+-MSL x2) DMS/ DMC	2021?	N/A	26	1,046/ 2,092hp	100mph
197	CAF	LD	2/3	DMSL MSL DMS/ DMC	2021?	N/A	77	1,046hp	100mph

Above: 139001 approaches Stourbridge Junction on 29 September 2020 on 2P78, the 12.10 from Stourbridge Town. The Class 139 Parry People Movers were built in 2008 exclusively for use on the self-contained Stourbridge Junction to Stourbridge Town branch. Entering service in 2009, the two units replaced the previously used Class 153 and remain in use. The duo are housed in a shed on the down side of Platform 1, which is exclusive for branch trains. The units use a flywheel to store energy (recharged from braking) and topped up by a small 86hp onboard liquid petroleum gas power unit.

Left: 165037 approaches Kings Sutton in June 2000 on a Banbury to London Marylebone stopping service. 39 of the 75mph Class 165/0s and 37 of the 90mph Class 165/1s were built, both in two- and three-car variants, at BREL York between 1990 and 1992. Together with the later Class 166s, the units are often referred to as 'Turbos' and operated over the Chiltern and Thames areas of Network SouthEast. Following the arrival of the Class 168s, the Chiltern '165/0s' are generally restricted to stopping services out of Marylebone. Meanwhile, following electrification of the Great Western Main Line, much of the Thames Valley '165' work has been taken over by Class 387s with many 'Turbos' now operating from the Bristol area.

21 of the three-car Class 166 'Turbos' were built by ABB at York Works between 1992 and 1993 as air-conditioned higher-speed variants of the earlier Class 165s. Like their sister units, the Class 166s have been largely displaced from Thames Valley workings, many sets moving to Bristol to increase capacity on services radiating from the city. In a scene almost unrecognisable today following electrification, Thames Trains-liveried 166216 arrives at Reading on a service from Oxford to Paddington on 15 June 2001.

The Class 168 'Clubmans' belong to the 'Turbostar' family, and they were built by Adtranz/Bombardier between 1998 and 2004. Nineteen of the three- or four-car sets are in use on Chiltern Railways services to Aylesbury, Oxford, Birmingham and Kidderminster. Four sub-classes exist: Class 168/0 (original body style), Class 168/1 (revised body style), Class 168/2 (with added exterior passenger information screens) and Class 168/3 (two-car sets modified from Class 170s transferred from TransPennine Express). On 24 July 2012, original series 168002 passes Kings Sutton on a London Marylebone to Birmingham Snow Hill service.

The Class 170s are a widespread DMU built by Bombardier Transportation (formerly Adtranz) at its Derby site. A total of 139 two- or three-car units were built, although nine of these were later converted to Class 168, and 11 were converted to Class 171. The Anglia franchise was won by National Express in 2004 and operated as One Anglia. The franchise used its inherited 'Turbostars' on Norwich to Cambridge, Bury St. Edmunds, Peterborough and Lowestoft services. These sets were replaced by the new Stadler 'FLIRT' Class 755 units at the end of 2019 and transferred to Transport for Wales. On 25 September 2005, 170270 arrives at Norwich on a service from Cambridge.

172340 pauses at Henley in Arden on 15 November 2020 on 2S47, the 13.57 Stourbridge Junction to Stratford-Upon Avon. West Midlands Railway has a fleet of 35 units in two- and three-car sets. The 27 Class 172/2 and 172/3s originally ordered by London Midland have 'Electrostar' style gangway connections while the two-car Class 172/0s, inherited from London Overground, are non-gangwayed. Chiltern Railways also operates a fleet of four two-car Class 172/1s.

On 12 August 2006, Class 175 'Coradia' 175110 in Arriva Trains Wales livery is seen near Llanelli on a morning Manchester Piccadilly to Milford Haven service. 27 of the two- and three-car sets were built by Alstom at Washwood Heath between 1999 and 2001 and the units have been in service since 2000. The whole fleet, now in use with Transport for Wales, is due to be replaced by Class 197 DMUs by 2023, though recent events may have delayed this schedule by a year.

51 of the three-car Class 185 'Desiro' units were built in Germany by Siemens between 2006 and 2007 for TransPennine Express. They have seen service over a wide area taking in Liverpool, Barrow, Windermere, Newcastle, Middlesbrough, Scarborough and Cleethorpes. For a time starting in 2007, the units even worked through services from Manchester Airport to Glasgow and Edinburgh. 185145 pauses at York on 6 February 2020 while working a Liverpool Lime Street to Scarborough TransPennine Express service. The units are gradually being replaced on these services by Class 68s and Mk.5 stock, these trains being marketed as 'Nova 3'.

On 15 November 2020, 196104 passes Henley-in-Arden on test and crew training duties, working 5Z24, the 13.39 Tyseley to Stratford-Upon-Avon, and return special working. The Class 196 'Civity' is another product from CAF of Spain, and is being largely assembled at Newport, South Wales, for West Midlands Railway. 26 sets are on order, comprising 14 four-car and 12 two-car sets. The units will replace the West Midlands operator's fleet of 23 Class 170/5 and 170/6 'Turbostars' and the remaining eight Class 153s.

Chapter 11

High-Speed Diesel Units

The first truly high-speed diesel units to run on Britain's railways in fleet service were the iconic Blue Pullmans in the early 1960s. They were clearly inspired by the success of luxury units like the continental Trans-European Expresses, which were designed to compete with shorter distance air travel. The trains represented another big leap forward in multiple unit technology, heralding the introduction of large-scale, high-speed DMU fleets beginning with the HST and leading to the 'Voyager', 'FLIRT' and IEP diesel and hybrid diesel and electric sets of today.

The Blue Pullmans would go on to provide a luxury service from London St Pancras to Manchester during the delays caused by the electrification of the West Coast Main Line and would also be used to provide a high-quality service out of Paddington for Bath, Bristol and South Wales. The new units were ground-breaking in many ways, featuring air braking, full air conditioning and distributed power. The Metropolitan-Cammell Carriage and Wagon Company-built sets utilised two German-built MAN 1,000hp power units, one in each driving power car, together with additional power units for onboard ancillary equipment.

Even though the Blue Pullmans only lasted in service until 1973, many lessons were learned from their design and operation, leading on to BR's own APT and HST designs; the HSTs being developed as far back as 1968 while the Pullmans were still in service. The APT, while it went into service as an EMU, was initially designed and run as a prototype self-propelled unit. The APT's origins pre-date that of the HST, perhaps to the opening of BR's Derby research laboratories in 1964 and work on improving rolling stock speeds up to a theoretical maximum of 140mph. At the same time, the design of a tilting vehicle with suitable wheel profiles and advanced suspension that could run round curves at a higher speed was under way. The research showed that the advances in technology would enable running of up to 155mph, although advances in signalling would be needed to operate in service at such speeds.

While HSTs are today often regarded as locomotive-hauled sets with the driving power cars classified as Class 43 locomotives, on their introduction in the 1970s they were firmly deemed to be multiple units, the prototypes being Class 252 and the production fleet being designated Class 253 on the Western Region and Class 254 on the Eastern. Today, high-speed units such as the Class 220 and 221 'Voyagers' have largely replaced locomotive-hauled coaches on most unelectrified main lines across the network.

High-Speed DMUs

TOPS Class	Builder	No. of Carriages	Introduced	Withdrawn	Sets Built	Power Output	Max. Speed
220	Bombardier	4	2001	n/a	34	750hp per vehicle	125mph
221	Bombardier	4/5	2002	n/a	44	750hp per vehicle	125mph
222	Bombardier	4/5/7	2004	n/a	27	750hp per vehicle	125mph
251/261	Metro-Cammell	2+6/8	1960	1973	5	1,000hp per power car	90mph
252	BR	2+9	1972	1982	1	2,250hp per power car	125mph
253	BR	2+5–9	1976	n/a	58	2,250hp per power car	125mph
254	BR	2+5–9	1977	n/a	36	2,250hp per power car	125mph

14 of the five-car Class 180 'Adelantes' were built by Alstom at Washwood Heath in 2001-02, originally for use by First Great Western to replace and/or augment HST services out of London Paddington. Their introduction into service was heavily delayed due to technical issues and eventually, by 2008, FGW returned the whole fleet back to the ROSCO, Angel Trains. Five eventually returned back to service with FGW after reliability modifications before being replaced by IEPs and transferred to Grand Central in 2017. Some sets were used by Northern between 2008 and 2011 with others being used by Hull Trains. 180105 leaves Bath Spa on 5 February 2002 on a Bristol Temple Meads to London Paddington service.

180105 stands at London King's Cross with a Grand Central service for Sunderland on 5 January 2019. The company received the ex-Great Western units from 2009 and the Heaton and Crofton-based units were initially renamed as 'Zephyrs', although later the term 'Adelante' was used once again. Grand Central now operates ten of the 14-strong Class 180 fleet with the remaining four sets now in use with East Midlands Railway, having replaced the six-car HSTs inherited from Grand Central.

On 14 September 2020, Class 220 'Voyager' 220018 leads Class 221 'Super Voyager' 221121 into Banbury on 1O20, the 13.27 Manchester Piccadilly to Bournemouth CrossCountry service. During the COVID-19 pandemic, many of CrossCountry's units were doubled-up to assist with social distancing onboard.

On 13 December 2001, a number of Class 221 vehicles are undergoing final assembly at Bombardier's Crofton plant, near Wakefield.

On 18 January 2013, 221121 pauses at Coventry in the middle of a snowstorm, working the delayed 1O24, the 15.27 Manchester Piccadilly to Bournemouth CrossCountry service.

An unidentified Class 222 'Meridian' unit passes Cossington, north of Leicester, on a Derby to London St Pancras working on 10 February 2007. The Class 222s are a development of the Class 220 and Class 221 'Voyagers' delivered for Virgin Trains cross-country and West Coast services. Introduced from 2004, four Class 222s originally saw use with Hull Trains, where they were termed 'Pioneers', before joining their 23 sisters on the Midland Main Line from 2009, these having the brand name 'Meridians'.

The iconic Metropolitan-Cammell Blue Pullman units of the 1960s would have been given the designation Class 251 if they had survived long enough into the 1970s to carry TOPS numbers. The intermediate stock between the end power cars was also provisionally allocated the TOPS designation of Class 261. A Blue Pullman set is seen at Wembley Hill on 2 May 1964 on a football special from Preston, bringing supporters for the FA Cup final featuring Preston against West Ham. (Andy Flowers Collection)

On their introduction, the HSTs were classified as DMUs as they were fixed formation sets with a power car at each end. The prototype set was different in cab design to the production series due to requirements for secondman provision in regular use. For a couple of years, prototype power car 41001, owned by the National Railway Museum, was restored for operational use on heritage railways. On 4 May 2019, the power car with its dedicated Mk.3 coaches is part of a bizarre cavalcade hauled by DRS dual-mode locomotive 88009 with 20031 and 47727 on the rear. The unlikely combination is passing the 'Top Field' (made famous by the film *The Railway Children*) between Haworth and Oxenhope on the Keighley and Worth Valley Railway.

Originally, the InterCity 125 HSTs were classified as Class 253 or Class 254 multiple units on the Western and Eastern Regions respectively. Even as the HST fleet is seeing out its last days in regular service, the debate still rages as to whether the train is a multiple unit or a locomotive-hauled train. In terms of the most unit-like HST, the dedicated Network Rail test train is possibly the best candidate today to be regarded as a pure unit. On 21 April 2020, the New Measurement Train (NMT), also known as the 'Flying Banana', passes Cathiron, north of Rugby, working 1Q28, a circular test train leaving the Derby Railway Technical Centre at 12.28 and heading down the West Coast Main Line via Tamworth. The NMT entered service in 2003 with power cars and a mix of Mk.2 and Mk.3 coaches, later becoming an all-Mk.3 formation.

Chapter 12

High-Speed EMUs

The first serious foray into the use of high-speed electric units in the UK were the APTs (Advanced Passenger Trains), specialist tilting trainsets designed by BR to increase speeds on the highly curvaceous West Coast Main Line. While the units were not a great success, they proved the concept of high-speed EMU use and also the tilt technology designed by BR. In many ways, the APTs were the forerunners of the Class 390 'Pendolinos' that now operate all high-speed services over the WCML.

The next major introduction of EMUs on Britain's railways were the Class 373 Eurostar sets designed for the Channel Tunnel services via High Speed 1 and the equivalent high-speed lines in Belgium and France. EMUs were the obvious choice for these services as the likes of the French TGV had proved the concept had worked well for many years, while the running of locomotive-hauled trains at speeds of 186mph had proven impractical due to adhesion and track damage issues.

The development of electrification, and the need to replace the ageing HST fleet, saw a new generation of EMUs introduced, the AT-300 Hitachi series (Classes 800, 801 and 802) now used on the East Coast Main Line, the Great Western Main Line and some TransPennine services. These new

The Class 370 Advanced Passenger Train (APT) was BR's attempt to introduce high-tech tilting EMUs onto the West Coast Main Line in the late 1970s and early 1980s. Only six of the seven-car train sets were built and introduced into service in 1979 with trains in service consisting of two of the sets formed back to back. After limited running on Glasgow to Euston services and a programme of test running, the fleet was withdrawn in 1986. However, many lessons were learnt that fed into the development of the later tilting EMUs, including the Class 390s. On 16 June 2002, a special event was arranged at the Crewe Heritage Centre to commemorate the introduction into service of the 'Pendolino' EMUs with Virgin Trains. The company sponsored the repaint of preserved APT set 370003 and arranged for new 'Pendolino' 390006 to be parked next to it on the main line as a photo opportunity. Chris Green, former head of Virgin Trains, is seen giving a speech during the event.

modern hybrid units are also set to replace the HSTs and 'Meridians' on the Midland Main Line in the next couple of years and also bring improvements to the West Coast route with Avanti.

With further decarbonisation of the railways and new high-speed lines such as HS2 being built and expanded, high-speed EMUs are likely to provide the major rolling stock for inter-city rail travel in the UK for the next few decades at least.

High-Speed EMUs

TOPS Class	Builder	No. of Carriages	Introduced	Sets Built	Power Output	Max. Speed
370	BREL Derby	14	1980	2	8,000hp	155mph
373	GEC-Alsthom, BN	2+14/18	1994	38	16,400hp	186mph
374	Siemens	2+16	2015	17	21,000hp	200mph
390	Alstom	9/11	2002	58	6,840/7,980hp	125mph
395	Hitachi	6	2009	29	4,480hp	140mph
800	Hitachi	5/9	2017	93	3,600/6,000hp	125mph
801	Hitachi	5/9	2019	42	3,600/6,000hp	125mph
802	Hitachi	5/9	2018	60	3,600/6,000hp	125mph

North of London Class 373/3 Eurostar set 3306 stands at London King's Cross in 2003 on a working from Leeds. These internal Eurostar sets (3301-06) consisted of two power cars with 14 trailers and were finished in GNER vinyls. Some restrictions caused issues in terms of pathing the sets between the Class 91s at the time, including longer dwell times at stations (due to fewer doors on the articulated units) and a top speed of only 110mph south of Grantham (due to steep contact wire gradients and issues with the Eurostar pantographs set for 186mph running). When Class 91 availability returned to normal levels, the Eurostars were taken off lease in 2005 and used on domestic services in France.

On 11 April 2003, Eurostar set 3007 undergoes heavy maintenance at North Pole depot, adjacent to the Great Western Main Line. As can be seen, for logistical purposes the 20-carriage long Eurostar sets are split into two for maintenance. The depot was closed in 2007 after the movement of Eurostar's London terminus from Waterloo to St Pancras with a new depot provided at Temple Mills, near Stratford International, on the High Speed 1 route. Each of a Eurostar set's two power cars features a six-digit identifying number starting with 373. The initial '3' denotes that the train is a Mark 3 TGV (Mark 1s being SNCF TGV Sud-Est and Mark 2s are SNCF TGV Atlantique). The fourth digit on the power cars signifies the owning country as follows: UK – 3730xx, Belgium – 3731xx, France – 3732xx and Regional and North of London sets – 3733xx.

The Class 374 EMUs, branded as Eurostar e320, are 16-coach versions of the Siemens 'Velaro' family of high-speed units and were introduced in 2015 to replace, and add additional capacity to, the earlier Class 373 fleet. 17 of the sets were built between 2011 and 2018 to enable greater interoperability and through running to destinations in Germany and the Netherlands, including Frankfurt, Cologne and Amsterdam. On 2 October 2020, set 4030 (one of the second batch of seven units built between 2016 and 2018) waits in the rain, fenced off in the international platforms, at London St Pancras, ready for its next working, 9O32, the 14.31 to Paris Nord.

Shortly after the introduction of the new 'Pendolino' units in 2002, 390013 is seen undergoing a full body lift at the dedicated Manchester Traincare Centre, Alstom's maintenance facility at Longsight depot. The units, leased from Angel Trains, were the last to be assembled at Alstom's Washwood Heath plant before the site closed in 2005. Follow-on orders for new sets and vehicles were built in Italy.

On 29 November 2005, an unidentified Class 390 approaches Tile Hill on a Birmingham New Street to London Euston service. At this stage, the sets were still in Virgin Trains livery with full Virgin branding and still formed as nine-car sets. From 2012 onwards, many of the sets would be lengthened to 11 cars and redesignated as 390/1s. The initial order was for 53 sets, built between 2001 and 2004, with another four sets delivered between 2010 and 2012 as part of the order to lengthen the already built sets.

In the months after Avanti took over the West Coast Main Line franchise, an unidentified Class 390 'Pendolino' unit passes Cathiron, north of Rugby, on a Manchester Piccadilly to London Euston service. The Avanti franchise began in December 2019 and throughout 2020, the new company replaced the former Virgin Trains 'flowing silk' livery with its own colours, many sets running in plain unbranded white while the rebranding took place.

On 18 January 2013, 390121 pauses at Coventry in the middle of a snowstorm, working the delayed 1B70, the 16.50 Birmingham New Street to London Euston, unusually diverted into Platform 2 due to frozen points.

Class 395 sets 395017 and 395023 wait in the pouring rain at London St Pancras on 2 October 2020 on 1J34, the 13.12 to Margate. Suffice to say, with two six-car sets provided for the service, and during the second wave of COVID-19, plenty of seats were available, averaging around two passengers per carriage. 29 Class 395 'Javelin' EMUs, part of the 'A-Train' family of Japanese aluminium-bodied EMUs, have been supplied by Hitachi to Southeastern and they can operate at 140mph on HS1 or 100mph on the comparatively antiquated Southern Region third-rail system.

Class 745/0 745001 stands at London Liverpool Street on 2 October 2020 after arrival on 1B67, the 13.57 from Stansted Airport. The Class 745s were built by Stadler Rail at Bussnang, Switzerland between 2018 and 2020 and entered service in 2020, replacing the Class 90s and locomotive-hauled stock on Norwich to Liverpool Street services by the end of March the same year. 20 of the 12-car high speed intercity EMUs were ordered and the fleet is allocated to Norwich Crown Point depot. The Class 745/1s are intended for use on services to Stansted Airport.

On 20 August 2020, Class 800/0 800029 leaves Reading on 1A18, the 11.30 Bristol Temple Meads to London Paddington. On GWR, the units are branded as Intercity Express Trains (IET). 36 of the five-car Class 800/0s were supplied to the Great Western Railway franchise for use on services from Bristol and South Wales to Paddington.

LNER 'Azuma' ('East' in Japanese) Class 800/1 800111 stands at York on 7 November 2019 on a London King's Cross to Edinburgh service. 13 Class 800/1s and 10 Class 800/2s were built for East Coast use between 2014 and 2018. The 'Azumas', ordered originally for use by Virgin Trains East Coast, entered service in May 2019 on services between London, Newark and Lincoln, after the franchise was returned to government control. The new operator LNER retained the 'Azuma' brand name for use. The East Coast Class 800s entered service almost two years after their Great Western counterparts due to electromagnetic signalling interference issues but today are delivering a reliable service and have taken over all East Coast services north of York from the Class 91s and Mk.4 sets.

Above: On 14 November 2019, 802212 stands at York on 1P37, the 17.55 Liverpool Lime Street to Newcastle TransPennine Express service. TPE ordered 19 of the five-car Class 802/2s for its main route between Liverpool and Edinburgh via York and Newcastle. Originally designated Class 803, later '802/2', the fleet entered service with TPE in September 2019. The Class 802s are physically very similar to the Class 800s but feature three higher-powered 940hp diesel power units to cope with the steeper gradients encountered by TPE services.

Right: The Class 801s are members of the Hitachi A300 Intercity Express family, essentially being an EMU as opposed to the bi-mode Class 800s and 802s, although they are fitted with a 750hp MTU 1V 1600 R80L engine for emergency use during a loss of power in the overhead line. The Class 801s are only operated on the East Coast Main Line by LNER. 12 of the five-car Class 801/1s and 30 of the nine-car Class 801/2s were built between 2017 and 2020. On 9 October 2020, two Class 801 'Azumas' await departure from London King's Cross. On the left is 801215 with 1S13, the 11.00 to Edinburgh Waverley, and on the right, 801228 with the 1N83 11.06 to York.

Chapter 13

Departmental Units

The railway has a long tradition of reusing vehicles retired from frontline service with the civil engineers, research and other departments. The Southern Region was particularly keen to reuse its withdrawn stock with numerous third-rail EMUs and some former DEMU vehicles passing into departmental service. The vast majority of departmental units came from first generation DMU and EMU stock, particularly Class 121 and Class 122s used for sandite and route learning.

The practice of reusing withdrawn units for departmental purposes has declined somewhat under privatisation with more purpose-built stock now being employed, such as the Windhoff multi-purpose vehicles (MPVs). Initially, Railtrack, and then Network Rail, retained a number of vehicles but this has declined to a mere handful of units nowadays.

The subject of departmental units is a complex and interesting one, worthy of a book in its own right and I can only hope to cover a small fraction of their long and complex history here.

Serco-liveried departmental DMU 901001 stands at Westbury in March 1998. Converted in the late 1980s from a Class 101, the two renumbered power cars DB977391 and DB977392 were initially used as motive power for an ultrasonic test coach. Under Serco ownership, they took on a more general testing role and are seen formed either side of track recording coach DB999550. Once retired from service at the turn of the century, the two vehicles were acquired for spare parts and scrapped at the Churnet Valley Railway in 2012. (Andy Flowers Collection)

Track recording unit 950001 (cars DB999600 and DB999601) stands at Tyseley in its original BR departmental livery in June 1993. The unit was specially built at BREL York in 1987 as part of the Class 150/1 order and not, as is often assumed, converted later from an existing Class 150. On privatisation, the set was reliveried into Railtrack colours and after renationalisation, into all-over Network Rail yellow. As it is based on a light axle-load 'Sprinter' unit, this allows the set to operate over almost all of the rail network, including areas where higher axle-load locomotives (as used on most departmental workings) are not permitted. The unit remains in service today, still owned by Network Rail and operated by DB Schenker. (Andy Flowers Collection)

Departmental and Service Units

DMUs/DEMUs

Class	No. of Carriages	Consist	Introduced	Withdrawn	Sets Built/converted	Details
901	2/3	DM (+-T) DM	2004	2012	2	Former Class 101 test trains
930	3	DM T DM	1993	1997	1	Ex-Class 205, ex-Class 951, Sandite or de-icing unit
950	2	DMSL DMS	1987	n/a	1	Purpose-built track assessment unit based on Class 150
951	2/3	DM T DM/DT	1986	1998	5	Ex-DEMUs for various departmental duties
960	1/3	Various	1992	n/a	28	General ex-DMUs (departmental use)

EMUs

Class	No. of Carriages	Consist	Introduced	Withdrawn	Sets Built	Details
910	Various	Various	2001	n/a	4	Former Gatwick Express Class 488 (ex-Mark 2 stock)
920	3	DMSO MSO DMSO	1971	1980	3	3-PEP Prototype Unit (ex-Class 446)
930	Various	Various	1945	2004	65	Wide range of Southern Region ex-EMU departmentals
931	Various	Various	1970	2004	19	Southern Region ex-EMUs for route learning and storage
932	Various	Various	1961	n/a	23	Southern Region ex-EMUs for research and tractor units
933	3/4	DM T (+-T) DM	1956	1992	4	Southern Region ex-EMUs for Mobile Instruction Units
935	4	DMSO MSO MSO DMSO	1971	1980	3	4-PEP Prototype Unit (ex-Class 445)
936	2/3	DM/DT or DT M DT	1984	2002	5	EMUs not ex-Southern Region (Classes 311 and 501)
937	3	DT M DT	1988	2001	6	AC EMUs, (Classes 302, 305 308)
960	4	DMSO MSO MSO DMSO	2001	2005	3	EMUs rebuilt as test trains

BR-designated DMUs transferred for departmental use as Class 960, together with EMUs reused as testbeds. The units were generally used for route learning, track inspection and/or sandite application, with a smaller number used for specific duties, including ex-Class 121s rebuilt as the Severn Tunnel Emergency Train. Class 122 55019 was transferred to departmental stock as early as November 1969 and was used for crew training at Preston and Carlisle. Under Railtrack ownership, the unit was used as a sandite application vehicle and during a major overhaul in 2004, the vehicle was repainted into all-over Network Rail yellow livery. In May 2005, 960015 is seen stabled at Aylesbury. 55019 is now preserved and awaiting restoration at the Llanelli and Myndd Mawr Railway. (Andy Flowers Collection)

977968 stands at Rugby on 1 May 2002, having been converted from Class 121 55029 in February 2002. Again designated as a Class 960, it was operated by Eurailscout GB as a track recording camera unit, this company being a joint venture between GTRM and Dutch/German firm Eurailscout. From 2005, the set was used by Carillion for driver and route training purposes. The unit is now preserved at the Rushden, Higham and Wellingborough Railway since 2010, after a period of storage at Rugby.

Further reading from KEY